W9-DIP-214

Retirement

Careers

DeLoss L. Marsh

Distributed by

CAREER RESEARCH & TESTING
2005 Hamilton Ave., Suite 250
San Jose, California 95125
(408) 559-4945

Copyright © 1991 by DeLoss L. Marsh

All rights reserved.
No portion of this book may be reproduced
mechanically, electronically, or by any other
means including photocopying without written
permission of the publisher.

Library of Congress
Cataloging-in-Publication Data
Marsh, DeLoss L., 1926-
    Retirement careers: combining the best of work and leisure /
DeLoss L. Marsh.
      p. cm.
    Includes bibliographical references.
    ISBN 0-913589-55-1 : $10.95
    1. Retirees – Employment. 2. Leisure I. Title.
HD6279.M37   1991
331.7'02'0846 – dc20   91-2036
                                          CIP

Cover design: Trezzo-Braren Studio
Typography: Superior Type
Printing: Capital City Press
Williamson Publishing Co.
Charlotte, Vermont 05445
Manufactured in the United States of America
10 9 8 7 6 5 4 3 2

Notice: The information contained in this book is true,
complete and accurate to the best of our knowledge.
All recommendations and suggestions are made
without any guarantees on the part of the author or Williamson
Publishing. The author and publisher
disclaim all liability incurred in connection with the
use of this information.

Contents

Preface

I retired at age fifty-five and by the time this book was published I had been retired for ten years. During the 1980s the average retirement age dropped to a low of sixty-two. A younger retirement age and an increased life span following the nation's greatest growth period has resulted in the youngest, the healthiest, and the most financially secure group of retirees in history. We are a skilled, experienced, and competitive group, many of us at the zenith of our capabilities. Age does not dull our need for competitive achievement nor our need to set and achieve worthwhile goals.

Of course, not everyone retires financially well off, but most people have some retirement income. I was a grasshopper, not an ant. I played when I should have been preparing for "winter." I relied solely on my retirement pension instead of developing my own program for retirement. My pension proved adequate for day-to-day living, but it did not leave much room for travel and other exciting activities. I do not regret being a grasshopper, for it taught me the value of diversity, and ultimately launched my exciting retirement career as a writer. I now enjoy the best of retirement and a career.

Much has been written to guide the retiree toward a financially secure retirement — how to invest funds for retirement and how to manage them once retired. These, of course, are very necessary concerns. This is not one of those books. The comforting cloak of financial security is not enough. You need the stimulus of a meaningful existence to be a whole person. Once your survival needs have been met, you need to satisfy your psychological needs, those needs of the mind that drive us all toward our own level of self-worth and well being. Satisfying your psychological needs along with advice for meeting your extra income needs during retirement are what this book is all about. The title says it best, *Retirement Careers: Combining the Best of Work & Leisure.* The book guides you toward making a career out of retirement to achieve an exciting new lifestyle, balancing meaningful activity with recreation and leisure.

The book's chapters are presented in logical order; however, each is an entity, allowing readers to skip about if they so choose.

The first chapter, "Why You Need a Retirement Career," emphasizes that meaningful, worthwhile activity is essential for a satisfying existence. Those who turn to a life of leisure without it often find retirement unbearable. Retirees discover their retirement needs differ drastically from those of the wage earner. A satisfactory retirement career may not mean a traditional wage-earning job. Instead, the retirement career need only be one that presents a goal important enough to provide self-worth and give life meaning.

This opens many options never before available. A career may now be volunteer work, learning new, worthwhile skills, pursuing creative endeavors, consulting, a home-based business, a competitive activity or sport, temporary or part-time work, shared work, a traditional job, or a combination of several of these.

Chapter 2 reviews retirees' attitudes and problems and how they are perceived by the corporate world. It examines the retirees' problems of entering the foreign arena of leisure without work, the differing psychological needs of the four basic types of retirees, and the problems and solutions of older workers who must work to supplement their income. The chapter also probes the still discriminatory but slowly changing corporate attitude toward the older worker. Despite discrimination against this worker now, the future will be brighter. Some companies now seek, and all future companies will be seeking, older talents and offer alternatives such as working at home, working part-time, providing job-sharing and adjusting schedules with flex-time. The reader learns the four major retirement career areas that are free from discrimination because of age and overqualification, and that cover virtually every type of career.

Chapter 3, "Knowing What You Need and Want" and chapter 4, "Goals for Retirement Success," are the two most important chapters of the book. All the remaining chapters focus on them, and they form the foundation for retirement success. Goals become more important than ever for retirees entering this uncertain period of life, with the most traumatic changes ever experienced. Knowing what you truly like and want during retirement and establishing the goals to make it happen are paramount for a satisfying retirement career. You must accurately identify your true wants. We so often believe we want one thing; then, once it is attained, we find it wasn't what we wanted after all. These two chapters will help you to identify and set your goals.

Retirement is a new beginning, offering the unique opportunity to broaden your horizons with new knowledge, to keep you young of mind for starting anew. Many educational opportunities are geared especially for the mature adult. They include everything from formal university studies to the Elderhostel educational travel program. Chapter 5 helps you to find your learning niche to make your retirement the best it can be.

Chapter 6 is the chapter of discovery, to find those career and activity options that match your special repertoire of likes and skills discovered during chapter 3. The chapter explores the many ways to illuminate the multitude of choices that match the retirees mix of interests and skills. Often the most satisfying activity is discovered in the most unlikely of places.

Chapter 7 on networking is important whether you are starting a new career, returning to a prior one, or simply improving your social status. Networking is a present-day buzzword for something people have been doing since the dawn of time. Now, however, it has escalated to a fine art. To network effectively, you must learn the rules and learn how to listen. Also, not everyone is comfortable in the network environment. The chapter gives advice to the timid and the introverted.

Time is a most precious resource, but for the retiree it is important that use of time be balanced to permit accomplishing the things that make life more satisfying and pleasant. Time should not be obsessively managed for the sake of scheduling every waking minute and thus sucking all the joy out of living. Chapter 8, "Time: The Retiree's Most Precious Resource," shows you how to organize your time to accomplish those things most important to your well-being.

Chapters 9 and 10 are tutorials for sharpening the mature career seeker's job-finding skills. Pursuing a new career may still require the investment of time and money for gaining the new skills needed to succeed. And if the retiree intends to work for others, this also means relearning the job-hunting skills of writing resumes and being interviewed, with emphasis on countering discrimination because of age or overqualification.

Those returning to the traditional job market may be surprised to find writing resumes has changed drastically. Resumes are no longer a dry, monotonous list of jobs and responsibilities. Today's resumes are objective oriented, with the skills and accomplishments of the applicant described in terms important to the employer. Further, successful resumes follow tested advertising methods. Chapter 9 tells how.

Being interviewed is never fun, and most would almost rather suffer the flu than be interviewed. Interviewing seems to be a problem whether one is eight or eighty. It's a fact of work life: jobs, volunteer positions, and entrances to some professional and social organizations call for an interview. For securing a job, the interview is the most important and most frightening step in the job-finding process. Chapter 10, "Interviews: Your Final Frontier," holds the retiree's hand through the interview process and provides valuable advice and guidance to help take the chill out of the interview.

The last four chapters suggest retirement careers that are free from age or overqualification discrimination. They offer the greatest promise for the retiree who plans to begin or continue a career.

For those reentering the work force, temporary services agencies offer the retiree flexibility and broad job choices. Once suppliers of clerical help, the agencies now provide a broad range of professional, technical, and industrial services. Chapter 11 explores why and how temporary work is a boon to the retiree careerist.

Consulting allows professional and technical retirees to enjoy the best of their prior careers with the freedom of retirement. It allows them to continue to work in their old careers, often for the same employer. Chapter 12 examines consulting for the retiree. It tells how to get started, how to expand and consult for other companies, and how to make the most out of the prior career and still enjoy the benefits of retirement.

"Starting a Home Business" offers an exciting prospect for the retiree. Most people at some time in their lives dream of owning their own business. Retirement offers the opportunity to make the dream come true. Chapter 13 provides the advantages and guidance for operating a home-based business, giving you the control to make of it what you wish — a full or part-time operation.

Retirement is a time when people are free to give of themselves for volunteer work. Chapter 14 was saved for last because retirees in career activities may also wish to become volunteers. As people age they become more caring, more concerned about those less fortunate. Thus many volunteer to help others. There are other good reasons for volunteering. It can be an opportunity to gain new knowledge and experiences or even be the road to learning and pursuing a new career. Chapter 14 points the way for a successful trip up the volunteer pathway.

I invite you to find your own special retirement career.

Acknowledgements

To Sydney, my wife and best friend, without whose help and encouragement this book would never have been written.

Writing a book is not a solo venture. Many people become partners in providing material to fill the pages. The author is indebted to a great number of such partners and extends a special thanks to the following, who gave so unselfishly of their time, their knowledge, and their experiences:

Collette Abissi, IBM public relations; Anna Agell, director, Volunteer Center of Alameda County; Tony Ayres; Herbert Baum, director, Service Corps of Retired Executives (SCORE), San Francisco regional office; Betty Beckman, SEER volunteer teacher; Ginny Bindy; Steven Block, national RSVP; Joan Boomershine, branch manager, Thomas Temporaries; Cheryl Bowers, president, Career Development Institute, Inc.; Susan Breed, director, Contra Costa Suicide Intervention Grief Counselors; Ruth Buell, volunteer coordinator, Monterey Bay Aquarium; Jim Burgardt, president, 40-Plus, Oakland, California; Stan Butler; Walter Butler; Marie Caslin; Mal Citron; Ruth Clary; Ruth Cohen, literary agent; Kathleen Correia, Accounting Solutions; Mary Craft; Paula L. Davis, 40-Plus; Carl Ehmann, executive officer, Regional RSVP; Nancy Engle, director, HARD Little Theater; George Erb, marketing, Executive Service Corps (ESC); Bronwen Evans, test administrator, Johnson O'Connor Research Foundation; Dwayne Eskridge; Gary Fisher, 40-Plus; Bob Fry, Marketing, 40-Plus; Nancy J. Gill, 40-Plus; Harry Gordon; Howard and Dorothy Granger; Claire Herzog, coordinator, Senior Enrichment Educational Roles (SEER); Gene Holm, personnel director, IBM; Pete and Sharon Irish; Jack James, communications, Executive Service Corps (ESC); Gregory Johnston, IBM; Al Kuchin; Debra Labourette, Orcard Supply Hardware employment manager; Nancy Landauer, San Francisco director, Retired Senior Volunteer Program (RSVP); Libby and Lovell Langstroth;

Ben Laub, 40-Plus; Mary Lou Laubersher, peer counselor, Cambridge Community Center; Jessica Lipnack and Jeffrey Stamps, Networking Institute; Edna Maleson, public relations, Locum Tenens; Laural and Vince Maloney; Florence Mason; Beverly Melugin; John C. Crystal Center, New York; Daphne Miller; Dee Mosteller, my writing mentor; Bonnie Nash, president, Thomas Temporaries; Albert Newman; John Phillips, vice-chairman, National ESC, New York; Jim Pol; Linna Lee Pol; Harold Poole; Dale Posner, press relations, IBM; Joann Ruby, Senior Enriching Educational Roles (SEER); Ms. Schoenecker, personal development and career planning instructor, Ohlone Community College; Howard L. Shenson, CMC; Jean Shiffan, communications director, Theater Bay Area; Andrew Simpkins, 40-Plus; Florence Thomas; Myron Troyer, public relations manager, IBM; Vern and Helen Vanerwegen; Dorothy Victorino; Paul D. Wcislo, 40-Plus; Ed White; Jack and Susan Williamson of Williamson Publishing Company; Frank Wishom, 40-Plus; John Holland's Self-directed Search, Psychological Assessment Resources, Inc.; Educational Testing Service; Chronical Guidance Publications; University of California Extension; Chabot Community College; Alameda County Volunteer Program; PATCA Professional and Technical Consultant Association; American Consultants League; American Home Business Association; National Association of Temporary Services; Accountemps; Manpower; Corporate Staff; California Consulting Association, Inc.; Lawsmiths; Volunteer – The National Center Senior Retired Volunteer Program (Natl RSVP part of ACTION); National SCORE.

Chapter One

Why You Need

a Retirement Career

There is no medicine like hope, no incentive so great, and no tonic so powerful as expectation of something tomorrow. – O.S. Marden (1850-1924)

A sudden rise in the value of his stock portfolio and Mel Macon, fifty-six, shed the responsibility and stress of twenty-eight years in retail sales management. The freedom to get up late, read a book, or take long walks along the beach was a welcome change from the stress of bringing home the day's problems. For the first few months he reveled in it.

Then Mel developed a feeling that something was missing. He longed for the familiar give and take of the retail sales world, not the stress and responsibility of management but the satisfaction of serving the public. He also wished to continue to enjoy the new-found freedoms that retirement offered.

Through previous contacts, he secured a position in a beach front gift shop. Now part-time sales to tourists and part-time walks on the beach provide the best of retirement and work. He has never been happier.

After thirty years of sixty-hour work weeks struggling to make it big in the cement contracting business, Vince Horton retired to a life-long ambition to travel abroad. After ten months in Europe and the Mideast, he and his wife could hardly wait to get home.

They spent the next six months fixing up the house the way they never had time for in the past. Then Vince began to unravel with a feeling of listlessness and discontent. There was no reason to get up early and do – do what? Everything had already been done. Vince, recognizing his needs, went to night school to learn to be a real estate broker. Soon, to his deep satisfaction, what he had once hoped to make a career became his retirement career.

Mel and Vince discovered one of life's great ironies. The playwright George Bernard Shaw said it best: "A perpetual holiday is a good working definition of hell."

The Beginning, Not the End

They learned what more and more retirees are learning. Retirement need not mean the end of one's career life. Instead, it can provide options instead of have-tos for a career leading to a new and satisfying lifestyle that offers the best of retirement and career.

Are retirement and career a contradiction of terms? No. A satisfying retirement means recognizing and fulfilling one's psychological needs – the needs that keep one interested in life. And the pursuit of goals and a career satisfy those needs.

Webster's *New World Dictionary* defines retirement as "withdrawal from work or business because of age." We need a new definition for modern-day retirees, one that describes changing from a wage-earning lifestyle to one combining the best of career and leisure. Retiring in the modern sense no longer means retiring from life or from work. It means retiring from what was a responsible must-do to a meaningful fun-do – a choice never before available.

People have been retiring for years, so why the problem of retirement leisure only now? The answer is longevity. Today's early retirements coupled with a more healthy, active, and longer life span result in dynamic, skilled professionals and artisans leaving the mainstream work force at the zenith of their capabilities.

When Congress enacted the Social Security Act in 1935, the average life span for workers was less than sixty-two years. Often people failed to reach the retirement age. Many of those who did were burned out at sixty-five, content to rest out their few remaining years rocking on the porch, whittling or crocheting. Now, however, many retire at fifty-five or younger. Early retirements along with a current life expectancy of seventy-five and a predicted life span approaching the nineties during the next century present an entirely new scenario.

Leisure Is Not Enough

We each enter retirement as if we were the first to do so, expecting leisure to fill our days with satisfaction. Then we discover, as many before us have, that satisfaction comes not from leisure alone, but rather from those things that satisfy our psychological needs for having a reason for living.

Elvira Turner, a registered nurse for twenty years, inherited enough money at forty-five to do whatever she wished to for the rest of her life. She immediately retired to play out her lifelong fantasy to travel the world to gain new experiences. Elvira's travels turned out to be heady stuff except for one critical element. Her empathy for others and her caring nature – a natural part of her makeup – caused her to miss her nursing job. The final solution satisfied both nursing and travel. By becoming a volunteer rest home nurse, she gained the freedom to nurse part time and travel part time.

My own experience and interviews with many retirees confirmed that most people hold misconceptions about what would be a satisfying retirement. Leisure, travel, hobbies, and recreation are usually envisioned. While all are good retirement activities, they often fail to fulfill the retiree's psychological needs.

What are the psychological needs that contribute to our feeling of well-being and self-content? Having a reason for being and making a contribution are missed by most who retire. Happy, well-adjusted people need a reason for getting up each morning – the knowledge that what they do is important.

Once people meet their basic physical needs of food, shelter, sex, and companionship, their needs shift to a desire to contribute, to be recognized, and to succeed. Leisure cannot satisfy those needs. Leisure, defined as "free, unoccupied, spare time," is without goals and is irrelevant. Leisure finds its meaning through contrast with meaningful work. There is nothing wrong with leisure. We need healthy slices of it. It only becomes unacceptable when we commit ourselves to a total life of leisure. Many who have done so find retirement unbearable.

Performing a useful social function and doing something significant are the psychological nourishment the human psyche needs. Pleasure is not derived from activity or leisure, but rather from the accomplishment of meaningful pursuits. We are motivated by the successes of surmounting obstacles to achieve goals. Total retirement without important goals for achievement puts people beyond both failure and success. When people retire without important goals to achieve, they feel impotent at the loss of unfulfilled career goals and the abandonment of career skills developed over a lifetime. Our competitive spirit is inborn. It does not turn off when we reach a certain age nor when we retire. The competitive spirit remains with us all our lives. A retirement career provides the focus for satisfying our inborn competitive spirit and our psychological needs.

Why Leisure Fails

Many people look forward to retirement expecting to enjoy their favorite leisure activity full time – to travel, fish, be a beachcomber, play golf, sail, or pursue a cherished hobby. After a short time, they often discover their leisure activity has lost its appeal, and find themselves engaging in that favorite pastime less often than before retirement.

I held a dream for retirement – the dream of spending my days sailing my boat on San Francisco Bay. At work, when my stress level rose to dangerous heights, I would take a day off and go sailing to regain my perspective. Sailing was my catharsis. But after retirement, sailing became a major disappointment, failing to satisfy my expectations. It took the challenge of a new writing career to put meaning back into my life and to renew the joy of sailing.

I found my experience was not uncommon. My interviews with others uncovered similar experiences. Engineer Henry Faust escaped from his job at every opportunity to go fishing. An unexpected opportunity for early retirement arose, and Henry could hardly wait to make fishing an everyday event. It quickly dwindled to an occasional trip. Henry is now back doing consulting work for his old company. And guess what? His enthusiasm for fishing has returned.

I discovered numerous other examples: Jim the golfer, Alma the quilter, George the kayaker, Jane the traveler, Wayne the cabinetmaker, Ann the basket weaver.

Why do leisure activities often lose their appeal once people are retired? If an activity was used as a diversion and release from job stress in the days before retirement, most retirees find it fails to satisfy their psychological needs.

When working, the people used leisure as a therapy to take their minds off the stress of work. That changes upon retirement. Now the retirees need something of substance to be involved with, something important to do on a recurring basis, something that will contribute to society, something to get up for each morning.

A hobby or recreation can satisfy one's psychological needs only if the person establishes challenging goals for it. But this moves it from the escape category into the career category. If retirees do this, the activity will most likely satisfy their psychological needs.

My friend Stan enjoys sailboat racing. Since his retirement he has devoted all his effort to sharpening his sailing skills and practicing racing strategies. His goal is to be the best racer in his class of sailboat. He is enjoying his retirement to the fullest by making a career out of sailing.

Career Options

A retirement career is one in which the person strives toward a goal important enough to provide self-worth and give life meaning.

Today's options provide the best of retirement's freedoms coupled with the best of a career. Retirement provides opportunities never before available. Before, it was necessary to make a living; now it may no longer be so. Many people have a measure of financial independence when they retire. For those who are financially secure, personal achievement toward important goals may be all that is necessary for career satisfaction. The idea of an exciting new career doing what you have always wanted to may be the spark to add zest, make you stay active and vigorous.

Those with little or no income who must work will find greatest success working at something enjoyable instead of "just a job." If money is an important consideration, search out a satisfying career. Being retired allows one to be selective, to seek a career to enjoy and make money too, something a person would do even if not being paid for it.

Many career options are open to the retiree. Some of them are learning new career skills. Other possibilities are the creative arts, temporary, part-time or shared work, consulting, holding seminars, starting a home business, teaching a hobby, craft, skill, or profession, and volunteering.

■ **Going Back to School.** Age is not a barrier to learning, and going back to school can be a career in itself. Many retirees go back to school to explore new horizons or start new careers. Retirement opens the door of opportunity to learn new things, and America's educational system provides a cornucopia of subjects to choose from, both casual and serious. Retirees can go back to school to become a lawyer or to learn to paint a watercolor.

■ **The Creative Arts.** For those who yearn to be in the theater, to paint, sculpt, write, or take pictures, now is the time. Nothing is more rewarding to the ego than having creative talents recognized by others. It is true that man does not live by bread alone. We all need stroking, and having talents applauded by others is stroking of the highest order.

■ **Work in the Corporate World.** Good news for retirees who need or want to work: the corporate view of the aged worker is changing. Though prejudice still exists, some companies are beginning to look toward the gray population to fill its ranks. These changes are coming about because the previously favored eighteen- to thirty-five-year-olds are diminishing in numbers. According to the 1988 U.S. Statistical Abstract, in 1980 those eighteen to thirty-four years old represented 29.6 percent of the population. By the year 2000 they will account for only 21.7 percent, and the percentage will continue to drop. At the same time, people over fifty-five already exceed 20 percent of the population and are increasing at the rate of 700,000 a year. This came about because the Baby Boomers produced 44 percent fewer children than their parents. In 1986 the birth rate dropped to 1.8, the lowest ever for America. This trend will produce a shortage of younger workers. America will need older workers to stay in the work force longer.

■ **Part-Time Work.** Performing part-time work for a prior employer is becoming more and more popular. Many firms ask their retired employees to return to work part-time to fill in the gaps. They prefer them because they are experts at their jobs, know the company, and understand company policies. They have also found them to be absent less and more reliable than younger workers. And more and more companies are allowing several retired employees to share jobs, allowing them part-time work and part-time leisure. Many retirees want to work just enough to bring in extra dollars, but not enough to cut into their Social Security pensions.

■ **Temporary Work.** Once only providing clerical help, today's temporary help services cover the entire professional and industrial field of work. Temporary work is made to order for retirees who want to work for others and still maintain flexibility. This is a good place to use your skills or gain new ones. Many people register with several agencies at the same time, allowing themselves to be selective when work is offered. Temporary work is often the best way for retirees to begin a new career or continue an old one.

■ **Consulting.** One of the easiest way for professionals and technicians to exercise their career skills is through consulting. Many companies depend upon outside sources for special projects and work load fluctuations. Retirees are often preferred over others because they know the company and policies, and they understand the work. Then too, the company does not have to worry about worker's compensation, or health and retirement benefits.

Many professionals have developed a good reputation and valuable rapport with contacts throughout their career field. Those professionals find consulting an easy transition, offering the best of their old career with the flexibility to balance work and play.

■ **Home Business.** Many retirees begin new careers by turning hobbies or interests into profitable enterprises. A hobby or interest can be an excellent vehicle for launching a home-based business. Many have successfully done so. A home-based business gives the retiree control over how deeply to be involved, leaving room for other pursuits.

■ **Volunteering.** A Gallup Poll found that 55 percent of the country's adult population volunteer in some capacity during the year.

Freedom from work lifts the lid of opportunity for exploring the world of volunteering. Volunteer work is especially appealing to the retired. It allows them to put a lifetime of hard-won skills back to work, to provide a valuable public service, and to put meaning back into their lives. Also, this is an excellent way to gain new experiences and learn new skills – skills that may lead to a paid position.

■ **Teaching.** There are many opportunities for volunteer teachers in the public schools. Among them are tutoring students and teaching English as a second language. Whatever your skills are, there is a public school teaching need for it. A retiree's professional and technical skills are important to others. There are needs for adult classes on just about any professional or technical area you can imagine.

Many retirees possess sought-after "old world" craft skills. Witness the resurgence of sidewalk boutiques that have proliferated at urban malls and summer fairs. Here you will find a wealth of talents and creative products such as glass blowing, weaving, earthenware, jewelry, antiques, basket-making, leather crafts, furniture-making, cabinet work, flower arrangements, clothing, costumes, masks, toys, quilts, hats, paper-making, block printing, silk screening, painting, writing, poetry, and on and on. Put your expertise to work by conducting seminars or teaching adult classes in schools, senior centers, and other social groups.

Advantages of Retirees

In finding and holding a job, the retired job seeker has an enormous advantage over the wage earner. Most of the frightening risks of career change are no longer a threat.

The number one concern — financial loss — becomes a nonexistent worry or is considerably lessened if the retiree is financially secure. In fact, many of retirement age want to keep their earnings low enough so they won't reduce their Social Security benefits.

The retiree's attitude toward a retirement job may differ greatly from the one held when making a living was a prime motivator. Making a living means striving for the next rung on the corporate ladder, a constant stretch to reach ever higher. Retirees are freed from that need, along with the accompanying responsibility and stress. Remember Mel Macon? He purposely sought a retail sales clerk job instead of a management position. Overqualified? You bet, and that's just the way he wanted it. Many companies are beginning to recognize what retirees knew all along: being overqualified is not a problem with most retirees and can be a definite plus for the employer.

Job security and seniority are two major worries for the younger careerist. It is frightening to leave a comfortable career and start a new one, giving up years of seniority. Such concerns are lost on the retired because the job is less important than when it was an absolute must, and nothing is being given up.

When people change careers they lose benefits and often give up valuable perks. The person who changes jobs may lose much of the money and seniority toward a company retirement. Other losses may include company stock options, company-sponsored health plans, and for upper managers, perhaps the use of a company car, trips in the company jet, and other niceties corporations provide their favored employees. By contrast, retirees have nothing to lose and are likely to gain new benefits. Whatever is offered will be an addition to what they already have from retirement.

Retirees also have the freedom to choose when and where they work. This is especially true for those who work for temporary help services.

Even the fear of failure is less of a specter now than when economic survival was at stake.

Career Potential Less Important

The young career seekers must strive for careers matching their wants and skills, and offering longevity and future prospects. They must guard against moving into an area where opportunities are declining and must assess their prospects and willingness to pursue highly competitive careers.

In contrast, retirees may not be concerned with these issues. Frequently, they move into highly competitive careers with little or no chance for adequate financial compensation – careers in writing, poetry, painting, acting, and photography. Of course, those careers have the potential of being financially rewarding, but most are not and for many never will be. There is a sea of writers and artists all waiting to be discovered, but even the most talented need a bit of luck and a great deal of tenacity to become financially successful. The retiree artists and writers may be more interested in the ego-satisfying prospects of having their accomplishments recognized than in earning money. This is something the younger wage earner cannot afford.

Other retirees may be seeking a job to make a little extra money, or to learn something new, or perhaps they just want to get out and be with people. Whatever the reason, they have little concern for the long-term future career prospects.

Many retirees are driven by altruistic motives to help others, to make a difference in lives less fortunate than their own. Mary Thornton, a retired employment agency secretary, had this to say: "It grieved me to see intelligent people unable to read well enough to fill out a simple application form. I vowed to do something about it when I retired." Working through the local community recreation and educational department, she tutored functionally illiterate adults. Mary Thornton is making a difference.

A Gallup poll indicates that 57 percent of volunteers want to help the less fortunate. Helping others is strong medicine.

Careers satisfy psychological needs through the pursuit of significant achievements; in this way a retirement career may differ greatly from the traditional wage earner's career.

The ideal retirement career is striving toward a goal important enough to provide self-worth and give life meaning. This book is dedicated to helping the retired person discover, select, and start a satisfying retirement career, examining the opportunities and problems peculiar to those who have retired. Go forth with confidence.

Chapter Two

Attitudes:

Yours and Theirs

We work to become, not to acquire. – Elbert Hubbard (1859-1915)

To be successful in beginning a retirement career, you must under-stand both the corporate attitude toward the older worker and your own attitudes toward a new career. Your attitude shapes your response to the world around you. You become what your attitude projects, what you envision. Anton Chekhov, the famous Russian writer, made this pithy observation, "Man is what he believes."

Your View

The retirement experience is so foreign from your past daily work life, a lifestyle you spent a lifetime developing, that the sudden transition becomes a plunge in the snow following a hot sauna. Be assured of this: Retirement will be quite different from what you expected it to be.

View retirement as an opportunity to pursue new, significant goals. Think of it as a new beginning – the earned opportunity to plan for those things that will make this your greatest period on earth.

The past is behind you. What you wanted and needed before may no longer apply. The present is now your concern. Develop your retirement career based on your strengths, values, and needs today. Deal with yourself in the present to find success in retirement.

There is no single magic formula for a successful retirement. Retirement formulas are as varied as the needs of those who retire. Your retirement needs are driven by your background and by your current needs. Therefore, your problems and needs are unique to you. You will, however, fit into one of these four broad groups:

★ Those who need earnings to survive.

★ The financially secure who enjoyed activities and hobbies before retirement.

★ The financially secure who were immersed in their careers.

★ The movers and shakers of industry, the decision-makers, the power brokers, who feel impotent now they've been stripped of their power.

All in these groups share one thing in common: They need a reason to get up each day and do something that makes their lives worthwhile.

The attitudes and problems of those who must work to supplement their income differ markedly from those who are financially secure and need only the psychological benefits of a retirement career. The former must face day-to-day survival issues; the latter must join with the first group in trying to satisfy a yearning for the feeling of self-worth.

Attitudes, psychological needs, and problems differ greatly within the financially secure retirement community. Those professionals who were managers and entrepreneurs with great power and influence over people and events suffer the greatest when stripped of their clout, and are no longer a viable force making monumental decisions. They are the most vulnerable and desperately need a retirement career that presents important challenges. To that end, many find satisfaction through temporary executive help services, consulting, operating a home business, or executive volunteering.

By contrast, if you retire with adequate funds and have diverse interests, you will be the easiest to satisfy, for you have the most options available for balancing leisure and recreation with challenging activities.

If you retire at a very early age, you may encounter a strange phenomenon in the form of reverse discrimination from those in your peer group. They may consider your action an abandonment of a career at the height of your capabilities, and thus chastise you for quitting your career so early in life.

Dick O'Neill, a forty-five-year-old Silicon Valley company vice president, suffered the slings and arrows of friends and colleagues for retiring early. He and his wife were surprised by this negative reaction following his retirement to pursue other goals. They condemned him for quitting at what they considered the zenith of his career, which in their view was a waste. Of course, it wasn't a waste, because Dick gained the freedom to travel, gain new knowledge, do volunteer work in an exciting new field, and be a consultant performing the Silicon Valley work he did before retirement, but minus the stressful pressure. His peers should be so lucky.

The Corporate View

The older worker has been the sacrificial lamb to the corporate mergers, buy-outs, and takeovers of the eighties as industry looked to early retirements to reduce their work forces.

Mergers, takeovers, and "lean and mean" reorganizations so firms could compete with the Pacific Rim countries brought about the 1980s waves of layoffs and early retirements. These often resulted in cruel and unusual punishment of older workers. Many of the actions taken by industry were shortsighted, reducing ranks through eliminating older employees' jobs or forcing them into reduced, early retirements. Government surveys indicate over five million workers were displaced during the first five years of the 1980s.

The age discrimination seen in corporations has not yet melted away, but it will. Why? Because they need us.

Many companies are beginning to look toward the gray population to fill their ranks as the number of competent younger people grows smaller.

The greatest improvement is in the service sector. The temporary help service industry welcomes the retired and enthusiastically seeks retirees in all career areas. Fast food restaurants do the same thing.

Kentucky Fried Chicken, founded by Colonel Harland D. Sanders at age sixty-five, encourages the hiring of older people through a program called the Colonel's Tradition. The program is designed to bring older workers into the organization at all levels. McDonald's seeks retirees through advertising, and trains and rotates them through all positions. Retirees are allowed to work whatever hours they wish. Wendy's and Carl's Jr. have similar policies but apply them chiefly to part-time work. Burger King uses older workers part-time at the discretion of the individual store managers.

Ms. Debra Labourette, employment manager for thirty-four Orchard Supply Hardware stores (OSH) with headquarters in San Jose, California, prefers older workers for purely business reasons. She finds Orchard's customers believe the older salesperson is more knowledgeable and experienced in answering "do-it-yourself" project questions.

"We don't have any problems with retirees who are overqualified," Labourette said, "We understand that their needs and desires are much different now than before retirement."

OSH runs recruitment advertisements in senior and retirement publications.

The company's training program consists of formalized instruction from training videos and manuals complete with tests. Persons hired proceed at their own pace but are expected to be completely trained in six months.

The Corporate Approach

The older workers have become a corporate dilemma. On the one hand corporations target them for early retirements to reduce costs by eliminating their higher salaries, larger benefits, and more expensive perks. And on the other hand industry is faced with an ever-tightening younger labor pool to fill its ranks. This forces more and more companies to rely on outside services.

It's a mixed bag for the aging worker. The best and most qualified older employees are often forced out on early retirements for purely financial reasons in favor of the younger, less experienced, and less qualified worker.

Corporations take a different view when they solicit part-time and temporary workers and consulting services. Now they want and seek the older, more experienced, and qualified workers. These are the people they know can and will do the job most effectively. And although the short-term labor costs may be higher, they are cost effective because the company uses them only for the duration of the project, and is not responsible for expensive benefits.

The reduced labor pool, the cost of retirement entitlements, and the better health and longer life spans for those over sixty-five are forcing economists and the corporate world to rethink when people should retire.

The January 24, 1989 issue of *Financial World* questioned America's trend toward early retirement. Nearly half the men sixty-five and older were in the work force in 1948. In 1989, only 16 percent of that group were working. The reduced birth rate is shrinking the labor pool of those eighteen to twenty-four years old, which by 1995 will only represent 24.3 million people – a six million decline from 1980. Companies are already finding it difficult to hire qualified applicants. Labor shortages from now to the year 2000 will force industry to employ older workers much longer.

A U.S. Department of Labor study predicted a growing shortage of younger workers between now and the turn of the twenty-first century due to the graying of the baby boomers and the reduced birth rate. The median age of the work force will increase from thirty-six to thirty-nine by the year 2000, meaning that half the workers will be above the age of thirty-nine. There will be a million fewer workers between sixteen and twenty-four years of age and the number of workers over the age of fifty-five will grow significantly. The report laments the fact that the average retirement age has dropped to sixty-one. This brings the current private and public policies concerning the mismatch between early retirements and a shrinking younger work force into question.

The report went on to state, "Older workers are important to the success of American industry, not only as a resource for production, but also for the maturity and experience they bring to the work place."

The report recommended that industry could increase its shrinking labor pool by improving the employment opportunities for older workers through flexible schedules, job sharing, phased retirements, and the training of workers in new skills.

American industry's age discrimination will be forced to change as the labor pool crunch becomes ever tighter. However, as with any discrimination, individual managers interviewing for jobs may continue to hold a bias against older workers for some time to come. Despite this, age is not a debilitating factor in four career areas covering most careers. The four areas of opportunities for retirement careers are temporary and part-time work, consulting, home businesses, and volunteering.

Work and the Retiree

Fifty-four percent of persons of retirement age work for reasons other than money. This was one of the findings of a poll conducted by the American Association of Retired People and published in *Modern Maturity* in the January 1989 issue.

The 35,000 readers who responded said that writing was the best-loved retirement career and store clerking was the least loved.

The retirement occupations broke down by these percentages: office workers, 15; factory workers, drivers, and laborers, 14; executives and managers, 13; salespersons, 13; professionals, 12; mechanics and craftsmen, 11; food, health, and personal service workers,

11; farmers, foresters, and fishermen, 6; technicians, 2; others, 4.

People and the work itself were the two most liked things about second careers, and the lack of benefits and the work schedule were the two most disliked items. Many are forced to work by financial needs. A total of 37 percent received no private pension; 53 percent worked full-time; 40 percent worked less than thirty-five hours a week; and 7 percent worked some time during the year.

More women than men seek second careers, 51 percent to 49 percent. Women earn an average $6,650 a year compared to $9,100 averaged by men. More women than men work for money in jobs they dislike.

Sixty-six percent of retired career seekers had to learn something new for the retirement career; 6 percent learned to work with computers. Sixty-two percent work less and are earning less than in their previous best earning years. Others are making more than before, especially those who start their own businesses.

An American Association of Retired People survey found fifty- and sixty-year-old workers stayed with a company five times longer than those twenty to thirty years old. The survey also found that over one-third of their 19 million-plus members would prefer to work.

Retired women suffer the greatest financial pinch. They make up 72 percent of the retired poor. A 1989 Older Women's League (OWL) study found the income for women sixty-five and older and heads of households to be only 60 percent of that for men of the same age group. The study also found the median income for men and women sixty-five and older to be $11,854 to $6,734 respectively. More than 50 percent of the 1988 widows classified as below the poverty level were not poor before their husbands died. Fewer than 25 percent of the working women received private pension funds when they retired because they worked for small firms or in the service sector where retirement plans were unavailable.

Many of the problems facing women are the result of the way in which many pension plans are designed. If a retired couple lives on the pension from a male spouse and the wife dies first, the male continues to receive the full pension. However, when the wife survives her husband she may only receive half of the pension, which often forces her below the poverty line.

The Job Search

Your job search attitude is very important for maintaining your confidence and for cracking through any age discrimination barriers you may encounter. Keep a positive attitude at all times. Remember "I can" succeeds and "I can't" fails. Use your network of friends, relatives, and colleagues to get to the people who hire.

In interviews, show enthusiasm for the job and company. Let them know that you, as a retiree, are flexible, much more so than other job-seekers – flexible in scheduling, job-sharing, part-time work, salary, and job assignments. Make sure you let them know you are not mired in the past but are willing to learn and use the latest methods. Dispel any concern they may have about you working for someone younger. With a positive attitude you will prevail.

Finding work requires perseverance. It's a full-time job and should be approached that way. Spend a minimum of six hours a day looking for that job you want. Corporations aren't the only galaxies in the universe. Don't overlook the new star clusters, the small one-owner businesses with a couple dozen employees. They represent the majority of America's new businesses. They are generally more interested in your capabilities than in your age and are more likely to treat your background with the respect it deserves. You'll find approaching them face to face to be much more productive than a resume paper barrage, but leave them your resume after your interview as a reminder of what a great person you are for the job. Keep your options open and seek all those jobs that satisfy your likes, dislikes, and skills.

In March 1990, the Maturity News Service reported on the Commonwealth Fund survey of the job attitudes of 3,400 men and women over the age of fifty. It found that 75 percent were willing to forgo employer health insurance, 54 percent were willing to change careers and retrain, and 35 percent would accept lower status, pay, and hours of work.

They sought work for the following reasons: Needed money for essentials, 34 percent; needed money for medical expenses, 13 percent; wanted extra spending money, 17 percent; wanted to do something useful, 18 percent; other reasons, 18 percent.

How to Get a Job

What are the most successful ways to get a job? A Department of Labor study found employees of all ages secured jobs these ways: 48 percent through personal leads from friends, relatives, and colleagues, 24 percent through direct contact with employers, 6 percent from school placement centers, 5 percent from help wanted advertisements, 3 percent from public employment department services, 1 percent from private employment agencies, and 13 percent from all other miscellaneous methods.

A similar AARP survey of *Modern Maturity* readers over fifty uncovered these job-finding statistics: through friends and relatives, 26 percent; started own business, 18 percent; newspaper ads, 17 percent; applied directly to employer, 12 percent; returned to former employer, 8 percent; employment agency, 5 percent; other, 13 percent.

Note that in both surveys, using your network was found to be the most successful path to finding a job.

Help Is Available

A lot of help is out there for the older job seeker. Federal- and state-sponsored programs in every area of the country will aid you in your quest. People over age fifty-five with low incomes are taught job-hunting skills and receive on-the-job training by the federally sponsored Community Service Employment Program. Contact your local Agency on Aging in the telephone white pages. For qualified applicants over fifty-five, the federal Job Training Partnership Act (JTPA) teaches job hunters how to find jobs and offers job skills training. Call 1-800-FOR-A-JOB for a list of the agencies in your area.

All states have employment department offices located in most cities to aid the unemployed, and many offer job-search workshops and individual job counseling.

Community colleges are a great source for honing your job-seeking skills. They also can aid you in deciding what types of jobs are best for you through career planning courses.

Being around others in similar circumstances can provide the support and motivation to make it happen. For you professionals who are seeking a comeback, a membership in the private, non-profit, fifty-year-old 40-Plus club may be your best answer for getting back into the mainstream of your profession. Forty Plus is a nationwide organization that aids qualified unemployed executive and professional applicants to get reestablished. There are currently sixteen 40-Plus clubs, in Houston, Texas; Washington, D.C.; Oakland, Los Angeles, and Laguna Hills, California; Denver, Colorado Springs, and Fort Collins, Colorado; Chicago, Illinois; New York City and Buffalo, New York: Winston-Salem, North Carolina; Columbus, Ohio; Philadelphia, Pennsylvania; Honolulu, Hawaii, and Toronto, Canada.

To join, you must be forty or over and have averaged $30,000 or more in salary over the preceding three years. It's a no-nonsense, forty-hour-week job search, and includes workshops that address networking, resumes, interviewing, and the like. It's a structured self-help program in which members are taught by other members. Each member is required to volunteer eight hours a week to help run 40-Plus. New members are counseled by peer counselors and a professional counselor to examine their past and where they want to go next.

In the northern California chapter, the Monday morning meeting starts promptly at 9:00 A.M., and is the kickoff for another week of professional job-hunting. All participants report on what they've done toward getting a job during the past week. This is followed by committee meetings and a guest speaker. This chapter provides an answering service and allows free phone service for three area codes. Access to typewriters, personal computers, laser printers, copiers, and a fax machine gives the job-seeker all the necessary office facilities to support the job search.

Frank Wishom, a fifty-year-old ex-marketing executive, waited five months for the phone to ring offering him a job, but it didn't happen. One month after he joined the 40-Plus Club of Oakland, California, he became the chief executive officer of a new marketing organization put together by three innovative telecommunication, hardware, and software firms to collectively provide them marketing support. "Forty-Plus did two important things for me," he said, "It gave me a place to go to organize my job search, and the job search training put me on track."

Costs vary in the different chapters. For example, the northern California chapter has a $150 entrance fee and $65 monthly dues plus a material usage charge.

The California Employment Department (EDD) has a special program for professionals seeking work, called "Experience Unlimited." This is an EDD job club structured similar to the 40-Plus system but without costs. Call the Sacramento EDD office (916) 445-1952 for the job club nearest you. Check with your state's employment agency for the services it offers.

Operation Able (Ability Based on Long Experience) consists of community-based senior employment centers in a number of America's cities (see Resources).

AARP Works is the American Association of Retired People's employment planning program consisting of seven job-search workshops for senior job seekers. The program is available in many of the nation's larger cities and is being expanded to others. Write Work Force Education (see Resources).

Your library is another source to aid you. There are many excellent self-help job-search books available, such as *What Color Is Your*

Parachute, by Richard N. Bolles and Jack Falvey's *What's Next? Career Strategies After 35.*

The Arts

Many retirees are attracted to the arts, discovering the ego enrichment of having their talents applauded. If this appeals to you, now is the time to paint, write, craft, join a little theater, or get involved in some other activity. Use this opportunity to bask in the glory of your creative accomplishments. What greater thrill than to have others read what you have written, hang on their walls what you have painted, use what you have crafted, or applaud your characterization in a play?

Your local community college system is the logical place to begin your career in the arts. It provides classes in everything imaginable. Community centers and senior centers are also good sources for getting started. Check with your local librarian for support groups and associations you may wish to join. It helps to associate with others of similar interest. You learn and gain from their moral support and competition. We aspire to greater heights when associated with those more accomplished than we are.

You don't need to be financially rewarded to be successful in the arts. Many seek only the recognition and applause as payment.

A retired Los Angeles Water Company engineer, the father of twelve and an inveterate story teller, uses hand puppets to act out stories for his many grandchildren and their friends to enjoy.

An eighty-six-year-old retired Petaluma, California school teacher wrote four volumes of historical family memoirs covering her life as a legacy for her children and grandchildren.

A sixty-seven-year-old Silicon Valley analyst retired to the northern California Redwood Coast and makes beautiful one-of-a-kind jewelry using the lost wax process.

A retired civil servant became a successful theater and screen

character actor by putting to use statesman and diplomatic charac-
terizations garnered from a Foreign Service career.

Aspiring thespians should get involved in local little theater groups
by auditioning for the plays and musicals they present. Those
groups need many behind-the-scenes volunteers to fill technical
support positions for stage hands, seamstresses, spotlight operators,
stage set carpenters, and the like. For beginners, this provides an
excellent opportunity to see what's involved in theater production
and execution.

Nancy Engle, the Hayward, California, Area Recreational Department's
Little Theater director, believes little theater presents many opportunities for older actors and actresses. "We audition and cast the parts
by age whenever possible," she said, "and because there is a
preponderance of younger people trying out, there is little or no
competition for many of the roles requiring older people."

Most people believe they have a book to be written, the Great
American novel spanning their experiences, and why not? We were
depression children. We lived through three wars. We witnessed
communications leapfrog from the crystal set to instant world-wide
television. And we saw man leave his footprints on the moon. Our
tenure spans exciting periods of monumental change – memoirs
for great stories.

How do you get started as a writer? Take writing courses at your
local community college or community adult center. Subscribe to
writer's magazines such as *Writer's Digest* and *The Writer* (see
Resources).

The beauty of becoming a writer is that you have such lofty goals to
surmount, because good writing is difficult and perfect writing is
impossible.

In your search for your retirement career, avoid negative attitudes
and thoughts. Don't listen to other people's downers about their
failures to find their place in the sun. Don't believe that you can't get
what you want because you're too old. Know that being old can be
better. Be patient. Don't let your anger and frustration defeat you.

Remember, you are special. There is no one in the world exactly like you.

The remainder of this book is dedicated to helping you make retirement your most exciting career.

Chapter Three

Knowing What

You Need and Want

Every individual has a place to fill in the world and is important in some respect whether he chooses to be or not. — Nathaniel Hawthorne (1804-1864)

When you retire, your needs and interests may be quite different than before. It's important to define those shifting needs and interests because a satisfying retirement depends on it.

Knowing what you want and going after it is what life is all about. That's what makes living worthwhile, what puts the spice in the sauce of life. Retirement may, for the first time, give you the opportunity to choose what you really want to do. Don't waste it by failing to understand your new needs and values born of retirement. When you have discovered them, don't procrastinate in setting the goals necessary to satisfy them.

Chapters three and four are the two most important of this book. They form the nucleus for the remainder to revolve around. Your goals and interests are tied irrevocably to one another. Don't make the mistake so many have of saying to yourself, "Of course, I know what I want. I've always known." Take another look, an honest evaluation. You'll most likely find your needs have changed.

The Quiet Life — Maybe

Before retirement, Les MacCortle and his wife, Dora, spent their summers basking in the sun at a lake in warm central California.

For them, it was a welcome escape from San Francisco's cold summer fog.

Their retirement dream was for a small quiet community where they would relax in the sun, water ski, and enjoy evening barbecues with friends. Once retired, they sold their San Francisco home and bought a comfortable cottage on an unpopulated portion of the lake, complete with a dock and a boat for water skiing. As much as they enjoyed the hot central California climate, they missed the interaction of a bustling community. They began to dread the quiet days of doing nothing. What had been a pleasant escape when working had become a boring parade of sameness.

A self-assessment of their true wants uncovered both to be gregarious, outgoing people who thrived on mingling with people. To that end they relocated to a town across the lake. Each became active in the community, he in the politics of the water control board and she in various community projects, satisfying their true needs.

It's surprising how often people are wrong about what they want out of life, what's important to them. This is especially true for those who are about to retire. All too frequently retirees discover the recreation or hobby so diligently pursued when working loses its appeal when retired. Or perhaps they discover the dream of a little lake resort with boat rentals turns out to be a nightmare. Few people are completely aware of their own talents, skills, and needs so they fail to recognize which activities will provide fulfillment. It is equally important to realize those things you don't like to do, those irritants that spoil your day.

Take Stock of Yourself

Now that you are retired, more than ever you need to take a good hard look at what you are and what makes you feel good about yourself.

Thinking of myself as a very logical person, I took the self-administered *Test Your Own Job Aptitude* by James Barrett and Geoffrey Williams.

The aptitude test consisted of logical reasoning, verbal reasoning, numerical reasoning, abstract reasoning, technical skills, and clerical skills.

I was dismayed to learn my logic ability was barely average, and amazed to find I was exceptionally high in abstract reasoning. Upon reflection, it dawned on me why I frequently solved problems through oddball approaches. I had taken the path not dictated by logic, for often the logical path seemed difficult to achieve or conversely too pedestrian. The abstract approach frequently yielded innovative solutions that would never have been born through logic alone.

It's strange, but often we mature ones may be as unaware of our true strengths and Achilles' heels as our younger brethren. If you don't believe it is so, ask close friends and relatives to list how they view your greatest skills and strengths. The results may surprise you.

We retirees have one tremendous advantage. We have a lifetime of varied experiences to draw upon to review and analyze for defining all our true interests, skills, likes, and dislikes.

You need to examine your skills and interest inventories in minute detail to assure you will make retirement your most exciting career. For the first time in your life you may be free to strike out on a new path unfettered by the dictates of others, perhaps free from the economic pressures of survival. An opportunity to chase new dreams and conquer new exciting challenges lies ahead.

Your strengths and interests are your pathway to a successful retirement career. Knowing your needs, what you want and what's important to you, directs your goals toward personal satisfaction and contentment.

Your goals cannot be properly set until you accurately define what you want. Defining your wants means examining both your likes and your dislikes.

Ask yourself these questions. What do I do best? What am I good at? Bear in mind skills are skills regardless of how you got them, even if you were never paid for them. Volunteer work, church, PTA, League of Women Voters, experience gained as a home-maker, administering home finances, marketing, all are solid experiences. It's far more important how much you enjoyed what you did and how good you were at doing it than how you gained the experience.

Getting to Know Yourself

Here's a technique to help you to get in touch with your likes, dislikes, and skills. Before we start, let me review with you the three basic skill categories – skills dealing with data, people, and things.

Skills dealing with data are synthesizing, coordinating, organizing, planning, analyzing, evaluating, researching, compiling, computing, copying, and comparing.

Skills dealing with people include mentoring, negotiating, motivating, counseling, instructing, teaching, managing, supervising, persuading, speaking, serving, and helping.

Skills dealing with things are setting up, precision working, controlling, operating, manipulating, and handling.

Examine yourself as if you were someone else. Probe deeply, reviewing and analyzing all your activities, achievements, likes, and dislikes. And remember, it's important to know what you don't want as well as what you want. Here's how:

■ **Step 1.** Take two sheets of paper and make two lists, a "Love" list and a "Hate" list. Write short sentences describing each of your likes and dislikes on the appropriate list. Start each sentence with an action word. Keep the sentences concise and descriptive. Be specific. Don't just say, "I like people," but analyze and state what you like or dislike about dealing with people. Be honest with yourself. Put down exactly how you feel, not what you think others expect of you. Include the appropriate skill or attribute for each description. Also, write down a skill code for each description, using P for people, D for data, and T for things. (Remember the three general skill categories?)

Continue each list until you have exhausted all the "loves" and "hates" you can think of.

Here are two sample lists:

LOVE LIST

I like to ...	Skill or attribute	Data/People/Things
Write "how-to" articles/booklets, etc.	writing	D
Analyze information to determine what's important	analyzing	D
Organize information into properly ordered lists	organizing	D
Plan how to do or make things	planning	D
Develop new ideas (invent new things)	creating	D
Build things (one-time projects)	work with hands	T
Machine make new one-time items	machine ops	T
Develop new ways to do old jobs	creating	D
Conduct studies to improve operations	analyzing	D
Develop computer software	creating	D
Manage complex projects	managing	P
Plan lessons for formal classroom instruction	planning	D
Coordinate functions between groups	coordinating	D

HATE LIST

I don't like to ...	Skill or attribute	Data/People/Things
Perform repetitive tasks	repetition	T
Meet people one-on-one for first time	people contact	P

Attend affairs where I don't know anyone	people contact	P
Sell products to new customers face-to-face	people contact	P
Talk on the telephone	people contact	P
Be embarrassed in front of others	prestige	P
Work under close supervision	controlled	P
Perform tasks that are highly regimented	regimentation	T
Check long rows of figures for accuracy	detail	D
Perform unchallenging, uninteresting tasks	boredom	T
Negotiate with people	negotiate	P
Take unsatisfactory products back for replacement	negotiate	P
Use coupons for products or services	prestige	P
Be interviewed by others	controlled	P

■ **Step 2.** This step involves an activities list describing all of your work experiences, volunteer positions, hobbies, and recreational pursuits. This list serves a dual purpose. It will round out and complete your love and hate lists and provide the future copy for your personal advertising brochure, your resume.

In this list, describe each skill and accomplishment, using short sentences and action words. Each description should include the applicable skill. Begin by reviewing your work experiences, followed by volunteer work, recreational pursuits, hobbies, and any other abilities you may have acquired. Include all those great things you've done, all your outstanding accomplishments.

Here's an example of an activities list:

ACTIVITIES LIST

Activity	Skill or attribute
Wrote how-to articles, resumes, & classified ads	writing
Wrote sailing handbook	writing

Issued directives	writing
Wrote procedures	writing
Interviewed resume clients and sailors for handbook	interviewing
Analyzed interview data for resumes	analyzing
Organized resume data	organizing
Lectured job-finding seminar	public speaking
Researched writing assignment (sailing and job-finding)	researching
Designed/developed diving equipment (manufactured, sold equipment)	creative development
Designed/developed toys (for toy manufacturer)	creative development
Machined small plastic/metal parts for development	machining
Build/machine one-time items for own pleasure	working with hands
Repetitive production of diving equipment	repetitive production
Supervised ten people, planning/analysis in ADP	supervision
Department head of planning/analysis in ADP	supervised other managers
Trained numerous people implementing hardware/software	teaching
Instructed 24 classes in ignition analysis	teaching
Planned lesson plans for training/presentations	planning
Developed viewgraphs for presentations	planning
Made numerous presentations to managers and others	public speaking
Conducted meetings with peer/subordinates	communications
Developed computer programs as a project leader	supervising
Consultant representing local command to Chief of Naval Operations	consultant

Coordinated implementation of large-scale computer	coordinating
Coordinated DPD operations with programmers and users	coordinating
Managed installation of ADP at Lemoore/Moffett	managing
Managed design and implementation of software	managing
Managed conversion of software from one ADP to another	managing
Conducted ADP capacity studies and software efficiency studies	analyzing
Liaison between vendors and management	liaison
Analyzed/improved work processes & material flow	analyzing
Conduct surveys/establish work standards	analyzing
Received superior accomplishment award via quality salary increase, and letter of commendation for managing installation of complex ADP systems into two satellite organizations.	management/ achievement
Planned church Christmas party.	planning
Counseled teens as girls' camp counselor.	counseling
Analyzed costs for buying camp equipment.	analyzing
Supervised four students in the library.	supervising

■ **Step 3.** Review your activities list, placing a check mark opposite each activity you enjoyed. Look for items you liked that do not appear on your love list. Also look for similar items on the activities list that can be summarized into a single love entry. Continue comparing the activities list against the love list until you have identified and summarized all the activities you enjoyed doing. Repeat the same steps for reconciling the disliked activities against your hate list. By now you will have compiled a large number of likes and dislikes, setting the stage for self-analysis.

■ **Step 4.** Self-analysis requires the love and hate lists be arranged so items are listed in their importance to you, beginning with what you liked or disliked most.

One method of doing this is to number the entries in the desired priority, then rewrite them into the new numerical sequence. A better method is to cut out each entry with scissors and then rearrange them until you have arrived at the desired priority. This method allows you to try several sequences. Rewrite the revised lists into the new prioritized sequence.

■ **Step 5.** Knowledge of how well and to what degree your skills and preferences relate to data, people, and things is essential to successful career research. No one is completely oriented toward data, people, or things. We all have shadings of each with stronger preferences leaning in one direction or the other. Find the degree of your preference by calculating what percentage each of data, people, and things you prefer.

Count the total number of codes on your love list. Now, add up each code type separately, dividing each code type sum by the total for all codes. This will give the percentage of your preference for each skill area. Your hate list provides an inverse indication. As an example, if you have a total of twenty-eight items, and fourteen are data, seven are people, and seven are things, your preference is strongly data, with 50 percent. The remainder is equally divided, with 25 percent each for people and things.

■ **Step 6.** Harvest your top skills, as easy as picking apples from a tree. A review of your love and hate lists presents your transferable skills, ranked in order of the most liked and the most disliked.

You have identified your top major transferable skills and attributes. You have discovered your degree of proficiency for dealing with data, people, and things, and you know what you like, and just as important, what you don't like. This valuable knowledge provides the necessary tools to develop meaningful retirement career goals, goals that satisfy your psychological needs. And your knowledge of your transferable skills will aid you in pursuing those goals.

Other Self-Assessment Tests

A number of other free self-administered interest, skill, and personality tests are available. Check your local library for these excellent ones. You'll find them in the following books on career planning: *Discover What You're Best At* by Barry and Linda Gale, *Coming Alive from 9 to 5* by Betty Neville Michelozzi, *The Women's Job Search Handbook* by Gerri Bloomberg and Margaret Holden and self-analysis exercises by Richard Bolles in his breakthrough career book *What Color is Your Parachute?*

Another source for self-administered tests are modestly priced mail order testing services at Chronicle Guidance Publications (see Resources). Behaviordyne (see Resources) offers a vocational package that includes the Strong-Campbell Interest Inventory for $25. John Holland's Self-directed Search, a do-it-yourself test complete with instructions for scoring and analysis, is available for $5.50 from Psychological Assessment Resources (see Resources).

The Educational Testing Service has a workbook that assists homemakers and volunteers in translating those experiences into transferable career skills. *Have Skills Women's Workbook: Finding jobs using your homemaking and volunteer work experience* by Ruth B. Ekstrom, costs $7.95. The workbook was developed under a grant from the Women's Educational Equity Act Program to help women returning to paid employment.

Professional Testing

Not everyone has the patience or is objective enough to explore their own interests and skills through self-assessment. If you feel more comfortable in the hands of experts, several sophisticated, scientific techniques are available.

What can professional testing do for you? It can identify your strengths and weaknesses. The three types of tests most frequently used by career counselors are interest inventories, personality tests, and aptitude tests. Interest inventories measure your likes and dislikes and align them with compatible careers. They are not designed to uncover your skills or talents for specific tasks. Personality tests spotlight those personality traits and personal characteristics that help you to blossom in specific environments. Aptitude tests uncover your natural talents such as memory, reasoning, and the production of ideas. They do not measure values or skills developed through training or experience. In other words, unlike your experiences, your aptitudes test the same throughout your life. Johnson O'Connor is one of the best aptitude testers in the field.

Johns Hopkins University psychologist John L. Holland developed a popular occupational choice model consisting of six themes: social, realistic, investigative, artistic, enterprising, and conventional.

The themes embrace the following types of activities:

■ **Social.** People helpers such as teachers, psychologists, therapists.

■ **Realistic.** Technically and athletically inclined people such as skilled industrial workers, technicians, and farmers.

■ **Investigative.** Abstract problem solvers such as biologists and physicists.

■ **Artistic.** Idea creators such as artists and writers.

■ **Enterprising.** People influencers such as salespersons, politicians, and promoters.

■ **Conventional.** Data and detail people such as bookkeepers and financial analysts.

The nation's most commonly used vocational test, Strong-Campbell Interest Inventory (SCII), is a written test with 325 questions given by professionals to evaluate your interests directed toward those six themes. High scores in any theme suggest your stronger interest in careers or activities in those areas.

Other vocational tests include a computer-based interactive test, the

System of Interactive Guidance and Information (SIGI) available from Educational Testing Service, Princeton, NJ 08541; and the Kuder Occupational Interest Survey, available through college career guidance departments.

Knowing your personality type can guide you toward those activities and careers that complement it. For example, if you are an introvert, you probably would not feel comfortable supervising others. The Myers-Briggs Type Indicator (MBTI) is the test most often used to analyze your personality traits, those things that make you act and react the way you do.

The Myers-Briggs determines your personality type judged against the four scales of extroversion/introversion, sensing/intuition, thinking/feeling, and judgment/perception. The test relies upon your response to a series of questions such as: Do you let your head rule your heart or heart rule your head? Would you rather catch butterflies or mow the lawn? Accurate results depend upon the honesty of your responses and the skill of the interpreter.

Other personality tests include the Edwards Personal Preference Schedule and Strength Development Inventory.

Some vocational counselors prefer aptitude tests. Such tests use audio-visual and mechanical exercises in lieu of a written test. The exercises are task-oriented, using three-dimensional puzzles and the like.

The nonprofit Johnson O'Connor Research Foundation is a leading example of companies offering such testing. The group believes job satisfaction stems from using all your key aptitudes. It has found most of us have four to six strong ones. The tests are designed, through the aid of an analyst, to match your abilities to various kinds of work. Here is an example: Good three-dimensional visualization is an aptitude necessary for designers and engineers.

The tests also attempt to relate your personality to career fields. As an example, people with objective personalities are more apt to be comfortable working on group projects, while those with subjective personalities are more apt to enjoy working alone.

The Johnson O'Connor Research Foundation (212-838-0550) has testing centers in fifteen major U.S. cities. The nineteen tests take a day and a half and cost $450. Aptitude testing reveals natural abilities, strengths, and weaknesses.

Free or inexpensive services are available at community college and state university systems. Many community colleges provide without charge some type of computer-based interactive test system such as System of Interactive Guidance and Interest (SIGI), Quest, and Eureka. They also provide free career counseling. For a modest fee, both state and community colleges offer personal career planning courses which may include extensive interest/skill testing, self-assessment, and career exploration. State colleges and universities in some states are unfunded for testing and counseling other than registered students and alumni. Check the ones in your state.

Don't overlook your state employment agency. Most provide some type of career counseling.

Testing Accuracy

Testing accuracy depends on the degree of correlation to success of the factors being tested, the objectivity of the person taking the test, and the proper analysis and counseling by the test reviewer.

Many counselors believe the proper use of vocational testing is the best way to discover your true interests for career success. Others, however, oppose testing. Even some who use it caution that testing to plan a career is not a straightforward process. It requires careful analysis by an experienced professional in conjunction with your own self-assessment.

The John C. Crystal Center (see Resources) does not believe in testing but prefers personal self-assessment. The center provides workshops with four themes: Who am I? What is the truth about work-for-pay? What do I want? How do I do it? The workshop requires the participants to write an in-depth autobiography.

Transferable Skills

Transferable skills are skills and personal attributes used across career paths, from one job to the next. Many of your most valuable skills are transferable. Communication skills, for example, are extremely valuable to all careers and a primary consideration for many.

Everyone possesses two basic types of skills: adaptive and functional. Adaptive skills are personality traits, your personal characteristics that make you what you are. Some examples are creativity, self-motivation, persistence, assertiveness, cooperation, diplomacy, emotional stability, enthusiasm, honesty, initiative, resourcefulness, versatility, and punctuality.

Functional skills are the skills developed through experience. They fall into two classes: those that are specific to a given type of work or field and those that are transferable across jobs and career fields. A functional skill always requires an object such as teaching whom? what? selling what product? Operating what type of equipment? Doing what kind of construction?

Your most valuable skills are those that are transferable. All of your adaptive skills and many of your functional skills, such skills as communicating, researching, managing, organizing, and coordinating, are transferable.

Skills range from simple manual dexterity skills, such as buttoning a jacket, to complex creative and reasoning skills, such as designing and developing complicated computer software. Experts claim each of us has over 500 skills that vary in complexity and value in the job marketplace.

Transferable skills fall within six broad functional areas: sales, marketing, creative, production, finance, and administration. Don't confuse fields with functions. A field is a specific company's area of competition, such as manufacturing computers, publishing magazines, or providing health care. An example of function is administering nursing in health care.

Review the fields you've been involved in. Did you really enjoy them, or would you prefer to search out new fields? If you prefer new fields, now is the time to make the switch, when your options are the most open and you have the most flexibility for change.

Aptitudes and Skills

Don't confuse your natural aptitudes, discovered during testing, with full-fledged skills unless you are skilled in those areas. Unskilled aptitude leanings need to be honed into skills before you can market them. How to do this will be explained in chapter 5.

Now that you know what you really want, reevaluate your retirement goals.

Chapter Four

Goals for

Retirement Success

If you don't know where you are going, you will probably end up somewhere else. — Laurence J. Peter

Many people mistakenly abandon their goals when they retire. That's unfortunate because without purposeful challenges our lives become aimless. We need the challenge of overcoming obstacles to give purpose to our lives. Most of us are inherent goal-seekers. It's in our genes.

People who feel life is not worth living lack worthwhile personal goals. Now more than ever you need to set and pursue yours. Without them your psychological needs go unsatisfied. Goals provide direction and give you something to look forward to — a reason for living. This and the previous chapter are the trunk of your retirement satisfaction tree. Successive chapters form the branches.

Retirement's Challenges

Retirement brings a new challenge: It's the challenge to adapt to a new lifestyle, and one that may differ drastically from that which you spent a lifetime doing. Remember we're talking about your retirement career, a career important enough to provide self-worth and give life meaning. It may be going into a home-based business, volunteering to aid others, or a brand new career. Whatever it is, it must be important enough to you to keep your juices flowing.

A married retiree faces the sudden constant contact with a spouse, placing new pressures on the relationship. The pursuit of meaning-ful goals calms the stormy seas of a relationship by keeping you involved and allowing space for your spouse. As important as compatibility and sharing are to a relationship, each person needs time apart to pursue separate personal goals.

After receiving a substantial inheritance, Harold Pollard, a construction superintendent, retired early. He was unprepared for his sudden windfall but welcomed it with enthusiasm. At last, he said, he had an opportunity to take life easy and do nothing, to sleep late, and to no longer suffer the frustrations of commuting. Thirty-five years of getting up at five o'clock every morning were enough.

After several months, he and his wife were constantly at each other. They finally ended a twenty-six-year marriage. Harold became despondent; his retreat from a lifetime of directing others on complex construction projects left him stripped of the challenges of accomplishments. Retirement became unbearable.

Risk of Suicide

Retirement puts men at a greater risk for suicide. An American Association of Retired Persons (AARP) study found retired men have a suicide rate four times greater than the rate for those still in the work force. Women fare better, apparently making the transition more smoothly due to a better social network and their traditional role as homemakers.

Susan Breed, director of grief counseling for the Crisis and Suicide Intervention Center of Contra Costa County, California, says, "We find the person who has been the most successful in life and has solved problems suddenly can't solve some of the problems of aging and develops a sense that society is saying 'we don't have a place for you now.' The calls we get on the suicide hot line indicate that for people who don't serve a useful purpose and lack a reason to stay alive, suicide becomes an option."

For those without goals, retirement is not unlike dying. Often retirees progress through the steps experienced by the terminally ill. First they express denial that their retirement will be anything but great, professing sleeping late and leisure without worthwhile accomplishment are the greatest things since sliced bread. Then comes anger from the boredom of having nothing of substance to do. This is followed by depression born of the knowledge that the quality of a life of total leisure is unbearable. Finally, most accept that activity with a purpose is a necessity and take some action in that direction.

A satisfying retirement stems from knowing and doing what is important to you. The best way to accomplish this is by setting and pursuing personal goals. Without goals your efforts and directions are aimless, resulting in procrastination. With goals your direction is focused. You are busy doing specific things, living life to the fullest.

Before retirement your goals may have been to satisfy the outside influences generated by others such as parents, teachers, friends, a spouse, and children. We frequently pursue careers our parents believe we should have. Or we follow the path of a close and trusted friend. Once married and on the parenting trail, we are driven to succeed by the economic pressures of getting ahead to capture the American dream and all its accouterments.

When you retire you are cast adrift, free from the pressures to succeed, free to do as you wish, perhaps for the first time. Yesterday is gone. Don't dwell on the past. Your needs and opportunities are different now. Work with what you are. Deal with today's likes, dislikes, and needs. Accept that your goals may be different, even less ambitious. Don't accept or use other people's standards. Goals are a personal thing.

For many, setting and pursuing goals remain an enigma. They may never have consciously formulated goals beyond some vague expressions of a dreamed-of desire.

Clear, reachable, and vividly imagined goals form the pathway to retirement contentment. Also, goals are a relative of time management. Each supports and reinforces the other. Your time is a finite resource; therefore, you must examine each activity in relation to your goals. Make daily time management a part of your goal methodology.

Put purpose back into your life and set yourself up for success by following these guidelines for setting goals.

Guidelines for Setting Goals

■ **Evaluate your past.** For success, set your goals on what you're best at, what you enjoy. Ask yourself what is important to you. If it is not important enough to make you want to sacrifice to accomplish it, it may not be a good goal for you. Passions and goals are the Siamese twins of purposeful living. Find your true passions, then sculpture your goals to mirror them. Say to yourself, "This is what I really want and this is how I'm going to get it."

The more important the goal is to you, the more likely you are to reach it. Commitment is much easier when you are doing something you enjoy. Find out what turns you on, what touches your emotional buttons, then go for it.

■ **Make your goals worthy of you.** Goals should make you stretch. They should be meaningful, requiring the exercise of your capabilities in their attainment. Setting non-demanding goals leads to procrastination.

■ **Don't set unrealistic or unattainable goals.** They will be only dreams and fantasies, worse than no goals at all.

At age sixty-five, it may be realistic for you to set a goal to participate in the San Francisco Bay to Breakers Marathon. Many do. But it is very unrealistic to expect to win it. Even so, goals should be a challenge to make you stretch and grow. Attainability is an illusive thing.

History is rife with people reaching the unattainable. Each of you must judge for yourself what feels right for attainment. However, understand your limitations. Talent and age affect your goals. You must dwell on what you can do, not what you cannot do. This is based on your strengths, values, and needs now.

■ **Commitment begins by writing down your goals.** That's the first step toward attainment. Writing them down gives them substance, makes them real, and brings them to life for you. Once they are written you have made an investment, a challenging promise to be kept. Also, writing forces you to clarify your goals. Once you've written them down, it's easier to combine several goals into one and to identify and resolve conflicts between goals. Long-term goals are easily lost sight of unless written down and reviewed. Written goals should be reviewed daily to become a part of your time management do-lists.

Start by writing a small paragraph of what you want and when you want it. If you cannot say exactly what you hope to gain in a very concise statement, your chances of accomplishing it will prove difficult.

■ **Broadcast your goals to others.** Telling others what you are going to do pushes you to complete your goals. Social pressure is a great motivator. Sharing your intentions and your progress toward success keeps your goals on track.

Declaring my intentions to write this book gave me the necessary nudge to start it. And encouragement from my wife and friends was the prod to keep me on schedule. It was amazing how often I might have put off a day's work if it hadn't been for my verbal commitment. Telling the world helped me get the job done.

Announcing your goals and goal accomplishments to family and friends sets up your own rooting section to cheer you on to victory. The ego-satisfying applause of others is a great stimulus for success.

■ **Visualize your goals for success.** Your mind is a powerful tool for visualizing achievement. Many of the world's great philosophers proclaim that you are what you think you are. Dr. Maxwell Maltz, author of *Psycho-Cybernetics,* explains the subconscious mind cannot tell the difference between actual experiences and those vividly imagined. Put your subconscious mind to work to imagine yourself to success. Do so by envisioning yourself successfully attaining your goals.

■ **Develop goals that do not involve others, whenever possible.** Goals dependent on others are frequently doomed to failure. You lose the power to control a goal's destiny when its success is dependent on the actions of others. If your goal cannot be satisfied without help, motivate those involved with publicized commitments.

■ **Make your goals specific and measurable.** Focus your sights on the goal's bulls-eye to make a hit. Vague, unmeasurable goals are powerless.

It is difficult to reach vague goals because what is to be done is not clearly defined. For example, if your goal is to earn money in real estate, do not set a goal by saying, "I want to make lots of money." That's too unclear. Your more exact goal might be defined as, "My goal is to earn $12,000 this year by purchasing, upgrading, and reselling real estate." Such a goal is absolute with measurable values that can be completed within a given period of time. You gain confidence when reaching such goals, injecting enthusiasm for setting and achieving new ones.

Comedian Lily Tomlin once quipped, "Ever since I was a little girl, I always wanted to be somebody. Now I see I should have been more specific."

Get your goals into sharp focus with exact and measurable definitions — goals that motivate you to take action and provide direction for that action.

■ **Make your goals manageable.** Long-term major goals are difficult to keep in focus on a day-to-day basis. Break them down into manageable steps that can be taken daily. Set target dates for each step. You can do so by working backward from your major goal. Each step must have a reasonable due date and lead logically to the next step. Such scheduling can be incorporated into your daily time management do-list and increases your motivation and action for completion. Achieving a step bolsters your confidence in your ability to pursue successive ones.

After I retired, my goal was to become a recognized, successful writer. However, unless extraordinarily talented, one does not become an immediate success as a writer. There is the never-ending task of learning the craft of writing, constantly stretching to improve style and reader acceptance. There is the need to become hard-shelled and able to overcome the rejection of work by publishers, for rejection is a writer's crown of thorns afflicting even the most talented and successful. And there is the need to learn to direct one's effort toward success by researching what editors and readers want.

The point is, my long-term goal was not within my immediate grasp and could only be reached by establishing and pursuing an organized series of lesser goals inching toward my final long-term goal.

I began by submitting fillers to magazines, followed by sailing, travel, and nature articles in ever more prestigious publications. Originally my success was defined in terms of becoming published. As my writing successes grew, so grew my definition for success. Success in effect became a moving target. Each accomplishment raised my expectations and thus the next level for success became an ever higher level for attainment. The setting and achievement of my writing goals have made my retirement my most exciting career.

Devise a plan of action for achieving your retirement goals. Your major retirement goals are a hierarchy of subgoals each related to one another. The accomplishment of lower level subgoals must lead to the next level of subgoals and that to the next until your major goal is finally attained.

The very short-term subgoals are the power goals. They are the ones that drive the system, that make it all work because they are the ones that become a part of your daily do-list. The small goals are the stepping stones of the big ones.

Reward yourself when you meet a goal deadline. Of course, the reward should fit the goal. Give little rewards for minor goals, bigger rewards for more significant ones, and a blank check for the really major breakthroughs. I reward my larger goal successes with a bed and breakfast weekend on the beautiful northern California coast.

Small successes are rewarded with sleeping in instead of my usual 5 A.M. wake up. Establish your rewards when you set your goals.

■ **Set compatible goals; eliminate obsolete goals.** Incompatibility between goals creates conflicts preventing fulfillment. Your time available is limited, therefore you must decide which goals are compatible and important enough to seek. And goals should never be cast in concrete. When a goal is no longer relevant and important to you it should be dropped. It is folly to waste valuable time and energy chasing old invalid goals. "There is nothing permanent except change." (Heraclitus, 540-475 B.C.)

Review your goals often and revise them when needed. Goals will change as you and your needs change. The very act of using goals to get the things you want produces changes and raises your expectations on what you want and can achieve.

Fear of failure, not lack of knowledge or talent, holds most people back from attaining their goals. And surprisingly, fear of success can also inhibit goal attainment, for success demands reaching for new horizons. It means stretching for new heights when we may fear leaving the comfort of our present cocoon. If we don't try we don't have to be afraid.

Keys to Goals

Remember these three keys to successful goals:

★ Write out specific, attainable goals that reflect what is important to you.

★ Spell out the steps required to attain each goal.

★ Set realistic deadlines for each step.

Goals are what life is all about. Goals make being alive worthwhile. Everyone has goals, but not everyone fulfills them. Fulfill yours by applying these principles. Doing so will make your retirement more meaningful and satisfying.

Chapter Five

Learning New Things

The education of a man is never completed until he dies. — Robert E. Lee (1807-1870)

You are never too old to learn new things, to probe new frontiers. Stretching your intellect will keep you young of mind and spirit, two giant strides toward satisfying your psychological needs in retirement.

Now that you have set your retirement goals you will probably see the need for new knowledge so you can reach those goals. There are many educational opportunities available to satisfy your every need. They include state and private universities, community colleges, commercial courses, high school adult classes, community center adult classes, correspondence courses, the Elderhostel travel/education system — and don't overlook self-study. Many educational opportunities are geared directly toward more mature adults.

Probably not since you were a youngster, living at home, have you been free to attend day classes full time. Of course, the educational system also provides night classes for those who are busy during the day. Going back to school can be as formal or informal as you wish. The important thing is that you keep learning. Whatever you are interested in learning, there's a school that teaches it.

Formal Studies

Universities provide full-time courses leading to degrees. Perhaps you want to complete your work for a degree, go for your master's, or head in a new direction. Universities also provide extension courses for part-time students. Many such courses will point you toward new careers.

University extension courses provide access to courses representing all levels of learning from the lower division level to the professional. The University of California in Berkeley is a good example of such a program. UC Berkeley Extension is one of America's half-dozen most highly rated programs serving the public. It offers approximately 1,900 courses during the three-term year and each is available to any interested adult. More than 50,000 people take advantage of the UC Berkeley Extension system each year. Check with your local university for similar opportunities.

Community colleges present fully accredited courses with a wide range of educational opportunities, many designed for specific career areas. Additionally, they provide adult classes geared to making life more pleasant and interesting, offering ballroom dancing, aerobics, painting, and crafts. If you want to learn to maintain your own automobile, welding, or how to build a cabinet, you'll find it taught at the community colleges. Course costs are modest, usually only a small registration fee and expenses for class materials.

The *World Almanac* says there are 2314 colleges in the United States; more than half of them are four-year institutions. This bodes well for you, for it is likely there will be several you can choose from if you wish to expand your formal education.

Eighteen percent of the total U.S. population, 40,751,000 men and women, participate in adult education each year; 64.4 percent of the adult education subjects taken are career related. Adult classes are attended by 12 percent more women than men.

High schools and community centers offer adult classes in many subjects and crafts. These are generally night or summer classes. These are often free or very inexpensive.

Fran Dick, a seventy-seven-year-old grandmother, the oldest student ever to receive a high school diploma from the Dublin California adult education program, graduated from high school in 1990. A retired medical secretary for Oakland's Highland Hospital, Fran decided it was time to get her diploma.

Many fine commercial schools are available. Study the Yellow Pages of any large city's telephone book and you'll find an amazing number of commercially available career schools to teach you everything from computer graphics and desk top publishing to restaurant management.

Correspondence Courses

Even if you live out in the country, you can get a top quality education from one of the top schools in the country. The University of California at Berkeley offers its Lifelong Learning Correspondence Courses to people all over the world. Faculty instructors conduct these accredited courses. They average $250 and you are expected to complete one within a year. Students can take up to three courses concurrently. Over 200 courses are offered covering everything from anthropology to writing poetry. Write for a catalog from Lifelong Learning Independent Study (see Resources). Other university systems throughout the U.S. have similar programs. Contact a university in your state.

A number of accredited commercial correspondence school courses are available. Who hasn't seen the International Correspondence School (see Resources) or NRI School advertisements in their favorite magazine? ICS courses lead to associate degrees in business and technology. ICS also has career diploma programs in everything from A to Z.

If you have an interest in the arts you'll find mail order courses to help you write, paint pictures, or compose songs. For example, *Writer's Digest,* a magazine aiding writers to become published, offers a correspondence writing course that monitors and guides the student writer's progress using experienced published writer/instructors.

Self-Study

Don't overlook the value of being self-taught through library research and networking people in your field of interest. Whatever your area of interest, you'll find associations and support groups that provide seminars and workshops covering it. Participation in such groups can prove to be very rewarding. *Gale's Encyclopedia of Associations,* in your local library's reference section, lists groups under every subject imaginable. And don't overlook asking around. Check with those who share your interest.

The library is an unparalleled classroom for gaining new knowledge. It requires initiative and discipline but a strong desire is an excellent motivator. Today's modern libraries maintain the latest reference materials, books, magazines, and newspapers on every conceivable subject.

Many different types of libraries are available to most people. Each is designed to better serve a given area of interest. For example, public libraries provide items of interest to satisfy the overall needs of most users. However, often in-depth information on some specialized subjects may not be covered completely, requiring pursuing the subject in a library that specializes in that subject matter.

Think of the public library as you would a doctor who is a general practitioner. He can handle the normal health problems, but must refer patients to specialists for those outside his expertise. Some of the different libraries you should be aware of include public libraries, university and college libraries, business libraries, and a number of special libraries.

The special libraries are devoted to specific subjects and funded and operated by private groups or enterprises. The *American Library Directory,* published by R.R. Bowker and available at your library, lists more than 30,000 libraries of all types. The listings provide sufficient information for you to decide if a query for information would be worth your while. Ask your librarian for other suggestions in locating the specialized information.

Researching and finding things in the library require an organized approach. First visit your local public library and get to know the professional experienced librarians. They are your most important guides for seeking self-help knowledge.

Librarians are required to serve the public. They deal with a great many people every day, many who take their services for granted, often not even offering a simple thank you. Getting to know your librarians on a first-name basis and acknowledging their expertise will gain you valued allies who will be there when you need them.

If you don't already know it, learn how to use your local public library's system for finding what interests you. Older libraries maintain extensive card files, and more advanced libraries maintain the bulk of their information on a computerized data base accessed by computer terminals. Regardless of whether it's a manual or a computerized system, your search effort will be similar.

Your self-help interest in a given subject can best be satisfied by reading books and magazine and newspaper articles about the subject. R.R. Bowker's four-volume *Subject Guide to Books in Print* indexes and cross-references available book titles, and classifies them under more than 62,000 subject headings. A second book by R.R. Bowker, *Books in Print,* lists all the current available books by author and title. These books should be your starting point for locating the books still in print for you to study.

Magazine and newspaper articles provide the latest and most timely information on subjects of interest. Ask your librarian for the *Readers' Guide to Periodical Literature.* This guide is the single most complete source for locating articles published in most major American magazines and periodicals. It answers the question of what articles were published in which magazines. Often, many of these magazines can be found in your local library.

Newspaper articles from one of America's major newspapers are available by referring to the *New York Times Index.* This index contains brief summaries of articles arranged chronologically. The information includes date, page, and column numbers. This information source goes back to the early 1900s.

Modern libraries maintain large microfiche and microfilm files of articles from the *New York Times* and other major newspapers. Ask your librarian what's available and then learn how to access it.

The total and proper techniques for researching information far exceeds the scope of this chapter. I recommend the serious researcher purchase these two paperback books: *Finding Facts Fast* by Alden Todd, and *Research Made Easy* by Robert Matzen.

Learning through Travel

Many persons have successfully made learning through travel a satisfying retirement career.

Georgia Rafael, a lively octogenarian, has traveled extensively throughout the world, making travel a learning experience. Becoming widowed in 1961, she turned to travel for solace and new experiences. She traveled whenever her teaching job permitted. Since her retirement she has made a career of travel. A member of the Travel Century Club, she has visited more than 162 countries and hopes to reach 200.

Georgia doesn't travel just for the travel alone but rather for the new experiences and knowledge gained of other cultures. She has accumulated more than eighty slide show presentations and volunteers weekly to lecture in schools and senior centers on her world travels.

Her favorite travels are those aboard research vessels with naturalists observing and photographing nature subjects. She's made several trips to Baja and the birthing lagoons of the gray whales.

"There's something about looking directly into the eye of a big whale to realize they're not that different from us. It's a sobering experience," she said.

Elderhostel Program

The Elderhostel program (see Resources) combines learning with travel. Elderhostel describes itself this way: "An educational program for older adults who want to continue to expand their horizons and to develop new interests and enthusiasms. We're for elder citizens on the move, not just in terms of travel, but in terms of intellectual activity as well. Our commitment is to the belief that retirement does not represent an end to significant activity for older adults but a new beginning filled with opportunities and challenges."

Europe's youth hostels were the inspiration for Elderhostel. Founder Marty Knowlton established the first of the programs in 1975. More than 160,000 people participate each year in over 1,000 different educational settings throughout the world including forty foreign countries.

The programs are designed for older adults and are available to those sixty years of age and older including a companion as long as the companion is at least fifty years of age. The students live in a pleasant campus or other environment and when not in class are free to enjoy the recreational and cultural privileges of the host.

Available courses cover everything from gene cloning to ballroom dancing. Whatever your interest you'll most likely find it in the catalogue course description. Courses are nonaccredited and consist of liberal arts and science subjects. They are structured with the assumption that the students have had no prior knowledge of the subject. Exams are not given. The host institution determines its own curriculum of three courses it will offer. Each class is held approximately one and one-half hours daily. Most Elderhostel programs are one week long.

Students are required to take only one course but are encouraged to attend all three. Free time is scheduled. Most programs include extracurricular events and tours as part of the package.

Accommodations are simple but comfortable in keeping with the hostel tradition and to assure modest expenses. The average cost of an American seven-day stay is approximately $255. This includes six nights' lodging, all meals, three courses, and extra activities planned by the host hostel. Travel to the hostel is the responsibility of the participant and is not included in the cost.

The physical requirements of each hostel experience vary. Some require rigorous activity such as hiking steep trails or climbing long stairways; others are less challenging. Many will accommodate the physically handicapped.

The Elderhostel program is a great way to travel abroad. Whether that is your desire or not, the program is especially attractive to those who live alone, providing them an opportunity to travel and develop new relationships while gaining new knowledge.

My wife and I are eager participants. We try to go somewhere at least once a year. We have found the people who attend Elderhostels to be bright, active, and energetic, some in their upper eighties. It's exciting and comforting to be around people who are in their eighties, and find them to be vibrant and active participants in life, savoring every moment. Many make a career out of Elderhostel, traveling and learning as they go about America and the world meeting and enjoying new relationships. On our trip to the Skagit College Elderhostel on Lopez Island in the San Juans, we met a woman who had attended forty-five Elderhostels in twelve countries.

Starting Over

It's never too late to begin a new career. Many famous people have blossomed to prominence in their later years. Mother Teresa, Albert Schweitzer, and Mahatma Gandhi are internationally renowned examples. You don't have to become famous, however; you just have to be alive and interested in life's challenges to stride forward to new beginnings.

Selma Plaut, at 100 years of age, received her bachelor of arts degree from the University of Toronto at a graduation exercise in 1990. Selma is living proof it's never too late to go back to school.

After widowed Linda Leigh's children left the nest, she went back to school to attain a BS degree in industrial relations. It took her six years of night classes at the University of San Francisco while working. She graduated with a grade point average of 3.96, the highest in her industrial relations class and the second highest of the entire university. She received the Faculty Award for Excellence.

In 1980 Libby Langstroth, Ph.D., anthropologist, and Lovell Langstroth, M.D., retired to the Monterey Peninsula. They set new goals for a retirement career, one that took them far removed from past experiences to a new career working as partners in the exciting underwater world of marine biology and photography. They successfully completed a number of post-graduate marine biology courses from prestigious Stanford University Hopkins Marine Station and the California State Moss Landing Marine Laboratory. Since 1980, they have logged more than 500 photographic research dives around the Monterey Peninsula and have extensively photographed marine invertebrates throughout the Pacific and Caribbean.

Their work has been exhibited and received critical acclaim at a number of noted institutions: the California Academy of Sciences, San Francisco; the Lawrence Hall of Science, Berkeley; the Coyote Point Museum, San Mateo; the Pacific Grove Natural History Museum, and the Monterey Bay Aquarium. They have published articles in *Natural History* and *Pacific Discovery* magazines and fulfill lecture and slide show requests to university zoological departments and lay audiences.

Libby, at age sixty-nine, and Lovell, at age seventy-four, have proven it's never too late to change directions and pursue a new dream.

When asked, Lovell said, "I've never been happier or enjoyed life more."

Henry Ford once said, "Anyone who stops learning is old, whether at twenty or eighty. Anyone who keeps learning stays young. The greatest thing in life is to keep your mind young."

Keep your dream alive through furthering your knowledge.

Chapter Six

Matching Your Needs

to Your Career

The hardest thing to learn in life is which bridge to cross and which to burn. – David Russell

This is the chapter for discovery – to discover options that make your retirement your most exciting career. Matching your interests, likes, and dislikes with the various possibilities opens up a myriad of options you may never believed existed. The transferability of your special mix of skills makes this possible.

Few people are aware of the many career opportunities that match their individual skills/interest profile. This chapter will take you on a discovery tour to ferret out the many hidden choices open to you.

Look for activities within careers that use your favored skills and problems your skills can solve. Review those fields that will make you the happiest by meeting your likes and interests. Don't overlook the negatives, your dislikes; they are as important as those things you thrive on.

Where would you like to work? What kind of organization would appeal to you? What kind of a work environment do you prefer? Are you a loner or a people person? These are important questions to be answered as you match your skills and interests to a retirement career.

Talk with People

One of the quickest ways to jump-start your investigation is to ask friends, relatives, and casual acquaintances if they know of anyone in a career of your interest. You'd be amazed how quickly you can amass a list of names of those who work in areas important to you. It's like the classic domino affect, one person leads you to another person and that person to another person for as far as you wish to explore.

You'll find most people like to talk about what they do. Find out what their typical day is like. You need to know what special abilities are important for success. Find out what they already have discovered. There's no surer way to get the pulse of things than talking to those who are doing it. They can give you the good, the bad, and the ugly. Make up your own questionnaire to guide you when interviewing those who are in careers you find interesting. Be sure to include the things you detest doing along with the good stuff.

Are there other ways to find those people experienced in careers you are interested in? There are lots of ways. Look in the local telephone book Yellow Pages for companies and corporations. Check with local unions. Talk to college counselors. Visit your state's employment department. Check with trade and professional associations.

Once retired, I matched my interests to those various activities that I felt would provide me creative fulfillment, and decided writing was a prime candidate to satisfy those needs. A writer friend, later to become my mentor, suggested that I attend a writer's group open house and talk to those who write for a living. I talked to writers of all types, from writers of fiction to nonfiction and children's books to technical manuals. There were those who were doing quite well financially and those who were not, but all spoke enthusiastically of their writing and the ego satisfaction it gave them. That day a new writer was born, a writer unbloodied by the first of an avalanche of rejection slips in quest of that elusive first published article. As my skill grew, so grew the successes, each a savored milestone.

Get Help from Experts

Trade and professional societies are the best sources to find information on new fields. Ask your librarian for *Gale's Encyclopedia of Associations.* It contains information on over 25,000 groups and associations covering all fields of interest. The four-volume guide provides addresses and telephone numbers to connect you to a source of information on the specific areas you seek. When properly approached, they will provide you the contacts for the information you need.

Use your local community college system. College career counselors and career planning departments are a great aid for career guidance. They maintain a wealth of information on a large variety of careers and are in touch with the latest advances in the career guidance field.

Local community colleges can help you search for a match of your skills to many jobs. Most use some method of reconciling skills and interests to careers and many incorporate some type of computerized search system. For example, many community college career planning departments use the Eureka computerized occupational exploration tool for matching your interests and skills to jobs. The data base contains over 1,000 current, individual job descriptions with employment outlook and salary levels. Career seekers fill out a one-page form consisting of thirty-five skills they enjoy and are good at, and the system responds with jobs that use those skills.

The library is a valuable source of career information. Most libraries have a multitude of books on various occupations, and they maintain pamphlet files for specific occupations. Local librarians can be one of your best guides for helping you match your skills to a career. Ask them for help.

Department of Labor Publications

Two United States Department of Labor publications form the nucleus for researching career opportunities, *The Dictionary of Occupational Titles* (DOT) and *The Occupational Outlook Handbook.* Both of these valuable books are available in the reference section at most public and school libraries. Ask your local librarian for assistance in their use.

The careful analysis of your skills, aptitudes, interests, likes, and dislikes has set the scene for defining the type of career work that matches. Make a list of all the types of work you believe would satisfy your skills/interest analysis. Arrange the list in the order of preference. For help, secure a copy of the latest Outlook handbook at your local library. This is a good starting place to begin a search. The handbook is updated every two years and describes over 200 occupations, what the jobs consist of, where the work is performed, salaries, and the education and training required. This handbook also directs the reader to additional sources of information about occupations.

The dictionary of occupational titles contains more than 17,500 classified and described occupations, each with a unique occupational code and title. The nine-digit occupational code number consists of three sets of three digits each. The first set identifies the occupational group, the second set represents the primary skill requirements, and the final set differentiates that particular occupation from all others. Thus, the full nine digits yields a unique occupational code suitable for computerized processing.

There are three arrangements of occupational titles: Primary arrangement by occupational group, and supplementary arrangements by alphabetical index and by industry. The occupational classification system with its skill requirements assists in identifying career ladders and skill transfers within industries and among related technologies.

Your likes and dislikes and your transferable skills provide the keys for successful DOT career searching. This is where those People (P), Data (D), and Thing (T) codes appended to your love/hate lists become important. The middle set of the DOT's occupational code number, digits 4, 5, and 6, are the key digits for specific, primary skill requirements: digit 4 is the data skill code; digit 5 is the people skill code, and digit 6 is the things skill code.

Suppose your top skill is synthesizing and you prefer working with data in lieu of working with people and things. A DOT review of only one of nine occupational groups uncovered more than fifty occupations, from astronomer to public relations representative. Had we explored all nine occupational groups we probably would have discovered over 400 matches. Obviously your interest will not be the same for all possibilities; that's where your love and hate lists come into play.

Some of you used the John Holland Self-Directed Search (SDS) method of skill/interest assessment and determined your applicable three-letter Holland Code based on the three personality types you most closely resemble. You may now use that code to explore which of the 1,346 occupations found in the SDS Occupations Finder and Alphabetized Occupations Finder apply to you. The Occupations Finder's 1,346 occupations are keyed to the Holland code and the corresponding *Dictionary of Occupational Titles* code. The required educational levels are also indicated.

What's important here is the opportunity for discovering options that might be of interest to you, options you never would have been aware of without the DOT or the Occupation Finder. Perusing all those options that match your peculiar mix of interests, attributes, and skills might present you with your ideal retirement career. And as you will discover in later chapters, volunteering and temporary help services are two areas where it's often possible to more readily transfer your skills to a new career.

Once you have narrowed your career possibilities, interview people in the field of your interest as described earlier. This is particularly important for two reasons: You want to be absolutely certain your choices match your skills and your data, people, and things preference, and your likes and dislikes. Second, interviewing managers in your chosen field establishes valuable personal contacts for later selling yourself for the job you want.

What Does Tomorrow Bring?

Even if you are less concerned about the future prospects for your retirement career than younger job seekers, it is still worthwhile to know what's hot and what's not—the job trends of today and tomorrow. A review of what's happening in the marketplace gives you a crystal ball peek at what lies ahead for making better career decisions.

Mergers, takeovers, bankruptcies, and declining industries, the results of a shift from an industrialized society to a service economy, all have changed the way we work and the way we think about and approach our careers. The financial gains of early retirements have freed many productive and accomplished people to explore new career and entrepreneurial opportunities. These are the forces that lead to career changes in the 90s.

Trends

Automation of the work place will continue at an accelerated pace through robotics, artificial intelligence, and expanded computerization, eliminating more low-level jobs. However, jobs in the computer field will continue to increase at a high rate, expanding in all segments of the industry. These include design engineers, robotics designers, analysts, programmers, software manufacturers, operators, and maintenance technicians.

Many will need to upgrade their skills by retraining for computer-assisted manufacturing or specific technical skill training for entering entirely new careers. And education levels will become more important due to an overabundance of college graduates, resulting in higher education requirements to fill entry level jobs.

The decline in membership in labor unions will continue through the foreseeable future. Restructuring of core industries to survive in the new competitive and deregulated climate will further reduce blue-collar jobs. The lack of union clout may result in less security and smaller pay raises than in the past.

It's not all black, however. There are some very welcome signs for the employee's future. Restructuring of jobs will lead to more flexible job hours adjusted to accommodate employee preferences. Permanent part-time work and the practice of job-sharing will increase. Restructuring will dramatically increase the number of people working for the company from their homes at least part of the time. This trend will help relieve the commute problem. Future workers may have more say in the work place, more control over their jobs through concepts such as quality control circles, a structured system whereby workers and managers form a team to improve the quality of the product or services and the efficiency of the system.

The service sector will continue to outgrow the manufacturing sector. Service industries are those not producing products or goods. Most experts define the service producing economy to include wholesale and retail trade, health services, business services, transportation, communications, utilities, government, the lodging industry, real estate, financial services, insurance, and personal services. Economists agree the service economy is much more varied and complex than previously considered.

The Occupational Outlook Handbook helps to more sharply define your final list of alternate career opportunities by examining future prospects for specific career types based upon projected population and industry profiles.

The greatest growth in jobs for the 90s will be for computer professionals, therapists, engineers, health service administrators, nurses, travel agents, preschool and elementary teachers, bank managers, accountants, and actuaries.

The more competitive jobs are for actors, writers, doctors, lawyers, stockbrokers, architects, designers, and real estate agents.

Declining and very competitive jobs are public relations workers, radio/TV announcers, chiropractors, dentists, social workers, economists, and high school/college teachers.

If you're like me you don't care if it's a highly competitive career or not. I'm only interested in satisfying my psychological needs to enjoy the time I have left. Money is not as important anymore. Maybe you feel the same way. If you do, go for it even if it's in a high-competition area.

Chapter Seven

Networking:
The Retiree's
Best Connection

Language is the light of the mind. – John Stewart Mill (1806-1873)

Networking is a basic human skill practiced since man first learned to speak. Every time you ask or answer a question you are networking.

We all gain from networking whether our interests are a new job, starting a business, volunteering, becoming successful in the arts, or just furthering ourselves socially. Networking is not just a tool to get a job or further a career. It's a valuable method for gaining information to help you in whatever your interests may be.

Many people are natural networkers, busy as bees flitting from flower to flower, gathering nectar and depositing pollen. Others need practice to learn networking skills, while still others are traumatized by the very prospect of purposefully seeking and encountering new relationships in search of information. Networking is different from asking for favors. It's giving as well as receiving information and advice. Successful networkers give as much as they receive.

All of us have a network and have been networking all our lives with family, friends, and the people we associate with in group activities. You have your own personal network and it is one of your most valuable possessions because you are most comfortable with it, and it has the broadest base of interests and people to draw upon. Your personal network is expanded by each new relationship you develop throughout your lifetime.

Produce Information

Networking produces information, and information is power. If you are seeking a job, referrals are your best source. If you are starting a home business, advice from those who are successful will give you the best information. Whatever your retirement needs, seeking out those in the know will give you the power for success.

For the retiree, networking is a great way to explore new retirement options. Seek out those people who have experience in the areas you think might interest you, then get their advice on where to go to get more information.

Frank and Elba Morgan retired to a new community 100 miles from a lifetime of friends and business contacts. Their move was prompted both for economic and aesthetic considerations. Frank wanted to put his real estate expertise to part-time use when he retired. He wanted just enough business to enjoy the work and make a little extra money for traveling abroad, something they both had always looked forward to. Joining the community church opened the door to other local organizations, resulting in a network of new friends and acquaintances that made their lives both a social and retirement business success.

"Without our involvement in community organizations, we wouldn't have been able to start our retirement business or enjoy the social life of our newfound friends," Elba said.

If you are a professional and would like to try something different, review areas of interest that parallel your professional skills.

The Langstroths, whom you met in chapter five, are a good example. Libby, the retired anthropologist, and Lovell, the retired physician, launched successful new careers in the study and photography of marine invertebrates. This has led to exhibiting, lecturing, and writing about this fascinating work.

Networking can be the salvation for those who retired with inadequate funds or had them whittled away by inflation. It can also help those widowed homemakers suddenly thrust unprepared upon the job market because of a reduced retirement annuity.

More people further their careers and start their first jobs through networking than any other way. These people find someone who knows the someone who can help them get what they want. Remember the Department of Labor Study? Forty-eight percent of all jobs are obtained through a personal network.

Networking is also for those of you who thought you had it all together by retiring to your favorite leisure activity, only to find it wanting.

In the previous chapter you searched for those activities that matched your interests, likes, and dislikes. Now you have the opportunity to put it to use by querying those who have been there. Join organizations or attend on a trial basis groups allied to those areas you think might interest you. Put to use your networking skills by following the advice in this chapter.

The Best Method

I talked to a number of 40-Plus members, a professional self-help club for job-seekers over forty. They all applauded networking as the most successful method for getting job interviews. Not all of them started out that way. Some started by answering ads and others by a paper barrage of cover letters and resumes. Most, however, failed to get interviews until they started networking. Some used their own personal network; one marketing executive gained a position by a referral from his banker. Others got interviews via participation in a professional or trade association. Still others developed contacts by talking to anybody and everybody who might know someone who can help them. Many researched managers in organizations of interest, then contacted them for informational interviews. This form of networking also often led to later referrals for job interviews.

Networking is people business. It's the business of making others look good and making them feel good about you so you can get what you want. You do this by showing interest in them, by appealing to their egos, by being sincere about their good qualities, by keeping your promises, and by being generous with "thank you."

Networking is the skill of stringing enough people contacts together to reach your objective. You can reach almost anyone by expanding from your existing base contacts. Don't underestimate the value of any contact. Everyone you meet has the power to lead you to others and that other may very well turn out to be your most valuable contact.

You gain by researching the groups of those who can help you the most. You already know where to find them. Remember? *Gale's Encyclopedia of Associations.*

Starting and expanding your network is easiest when you're not under the pressure of need. Having a network in place provides your entrance to a successful search when the need arises. This is especially true for you who are members of trade and professional associations that are interest- or career-specific.

Person-to-Person Networks

Jessica Lipnack and Jeffrey Stamps, founders of the Networking Institute, West Newton, MA, say networking has entered the lexicon to mean "making connections among peers." One person with a need contacts another person with a resource and networking begins.

Virginia Hine, anthropologist and networking scholar, says network units can best be described in one of these three ways: Self-sufficient, stand-alone units; decentralized units connected horizontally through overlapping membership and leadership; and units bonded together through shared values and ideas. Hine considers the bond of shared values to be the most important.

Segmentation allows one node of the network to function independently from other nodes. This explains why terrorist groups are so difficult to eradicate. Each group operates independently but with a common cause. A shared commitment to values, not objects, is the glue that binds networks together.

The independent network structure departs drastically from the common bureaucratic hierarchical structure of a top-down pyramid, rigidly designed for control at every level. Networks, unlike hierarchical organizations, have multiple leaders. Many in a network perform the functions of leaders, making it difficult to identify the true leaders. People in networks have dual functions such as to function as a self-sufficient entity (node) and to function as a member of the group (network).

Four Network Types

The four network classifications are vertical networks, vertical/ occupational networks, horizontal networks, and horizontal/occupational networks.

■ **Vertical networks** are similar to your personal network. They consist of a cross-section of people who have interests and experiences in all kinds of subjects. There are no limits to who would make up the network or what the subjects of interest would be.

■ **Vertical/occupational networks** encompass a certain field of interest. For example, you may be interested in writing and would therefore join a writers' association. Most writers' associations include all types of writers such as copy writers, technical writers, fiction writers, and nonfiction writers. Although there are distinct differences and problems associated with the different types of writing, such an association provides many opportunities for networking since all writers have many things in common. And of course you are free to seek out those within the association who share your particular interests.

■ **Horizontal networks** may cross all fields but are at the same level. A home business association would be a good example. Regardless of the type of home business you operated or were contemplating, you would share common problems with all other home business entrepreneurs. Networking in such an organization could steer you toward success in your own home business operation.

■ **Horizontal/occupational or professional networks** are the tightest, most focused networks of all. They target the same level within a specific field. Such networks offer the individual networker a bull's-eye instead of the whole target to shoot at. Suppose you are a writer of children's books. If you join a group of writers interested only in writing children's books, what they have to offer you and what you have to offer them are totally directed toward your common specific writing interests.

Be a Good Listener

Dee Mosteller, my mentor, is a natural networker. She can walk into a room and command the attention of all nearby. People seem to reach out and open their souls to her. She has that rare gift for making others feel important. They feel she really cares about what they have to say. She's a great listener.

The most successful networkers are people who have learned to listen with interest to other people. In networking as with selling, effective listening is the difference between success and failure. All successful salespeople are good effective listeners. That's how they get the pulse of the buyer and determine the buyer's emotional needs and what the buyer really wants. We buy from those we like and those we feel understand us – the people we trust.

In networking, we're selling ourselves to others. We're convincing them that we are someone who is a kindred spirit, someone who understands them, someone who is trustworthy, someone who is worthy of their support.

Show Interest

The best way to gain friends and establish valuable contacts is through the simple act of showing genuine interest in people. They are flattered to find you care about what they say and do, and they will respond to you in kind. Their attention to you is dependent upon your willingness to listen to them. Remember other people, like you, are more interested in themselves than they are in you. Therefore you can gain their interest best by showing interest in them.

Participation is the key to effective communication. Communication is most effective when it moves in both directions, each contributing and each listening to the other.

Don't start a relationship by talking about yourself. Find out what's important to the other person, what pushes his or her emotional buttons. All people have something that's very dear to them, the kind of work they do, a special accomplishment. It may be a favored hobby or a shared common interest. Listening begins with wanting to hear what they have to say. Be attentive and above all be sincere. Nothing will kill a relationship faster than false sincerity.

It pays to know something about a person beforehand. Do a bit of research on those with whom you hope to start a dialogue. Then begin by asking them specific, open-ended questions that require in-depth responses. Try questions beginning with what, how, and why. Such questions get people talking and revealing things about themselves that may be of interest to you.

Use questions such as these: What is your opinion about . . . ? What would you like to see done? What do you think is most important? Why? What kind of work do you do? How did you get in that line of work? What do you find the most rewarding about your job?

People enjoy talking about themselves and are especially gratified by those who show attentive interest in what they have to say and do. Shy away from asking questions that elicit one-word responses such as yes or no. You want to keep the communication channel open, and that is best done by questions that require a more involved answer. You also may learn facts that might not otherwise come to light.

President Lyndon Johnson, when he was a senator, kept a sign on his desk that said, "When you're talking, you aren't learning."

These are wise words we should all heed. Talking when I should have been listening has allowed many an important nugget of information to slip past me. I became painfully aware of this when copying the results of interviews from my tape recorder. I would often discover myself interrupting with an anecdote of my own, losing forever something important the person being interviewed was explaining.

Rules for a Good Listener

Everyone needs attention, and when someone genuinely shows interest in what we say and do, we react with friendliness. Being a good listener develops friendships and is the networker's most valuable asset. Here's how to be a good listener:

■ **Be interested.** Be attentive. Look directly at the person you are talking with. Give your full attention. Avoid distractions. Seek a quiet place free from interruptions and outside interference for your discussion.

■ **Never interrupt.** Interrupting the person talking may break the thread of continuity, resulting in the loss of valuable information. It is particularly inappropriate to interrupt with your own anecdote or opinion before the talker has finished. This indicates to the speaker you were not really paying attention nor interested in the speaker's opinions. Such actions may destroy your opportunity for future discussions.

■ **Don't change the subject** until you are comfortable it has been fully covered.

■ **Be sincere** in your responses to the speaker's statements. Use appropriate body language and facial expressions to indicate your full attention.

■ **Concentrate fully on the speaker.** Successful listeners force themselves to wipe their minds clean. Don't be formulating what you want to say next and thus tune out. This may cause you to miss valuable information, and it tells the speaker you are more interested in making an impression than in listening to what is being said.

■ **Don't anticipate** what the speaker is going to say. You may have your receiver turned off and miss something valuable to you.

■ **Concentrate on picking out the key words** and ideas being presented. Summarize the speaker's message for yourself. When the person finishes, recap what was said in a quick sentence or two. Using this technique forces you to maintain your full attention and assures you'll hear it all. When you're listening it's impossible to talk yourself out of a good relationship, and while the other person is answering questions, it's almost impossible for that person not to give you what you seek.

■ **Ask questions** to clarify anything not understood, but don't interrupt to do so. Wait your turn. Once the question is answered, repeat the answer so the speaker can correct it if necessary.

■ **Take notes immediately afterwards.** If you have a pocket recorder, use it to recap the key parts of the discussion.

Ten Steps for Networking

■ **Develop a plan.** Whatever your needs, they are best satisfied by developing a strategy. Your plan should include what you want to accomplish; what organizations or associations would best satisfy the plan's execution, researching those people you wish to contact within the organization; maintaining records of the results of each contact, and following through.

■ **Research the people you hope to contact.** Find out who does what and what their special area of expertise is. Find out what their main interest is so you can open the dialogue with something of interest to those from whom you seek advice or referral. People love to talk about those things that interest them the most. Find out what things you may share in common. Common interests go a long way toward kinsmanship, and such an interest can provide value to you both for future networking with one another. Remember that networking is a two-way street. You must be willing to give as well as receive.

■ **Be prepared to listen** and not dominate the conversation or bore those you wish to network with.

■ **Force yourself to circulate** among the members of an association or group. Ask everyone you meet what they do, where they've been, and who they know. Most will be glad to help you because people like the satisfaction of helping others. Introduce yourself, then ask open-ended questions that require thoughtful responses and that reveal something about the person. Try one of these: "How did you get started in your vocation?" "What do you find the most exciting thing about your job?" "What do you find the most irritating thing about your job?" Such questions get people talking about things they feel to be important and will open the door for you to solicit that which you are interested in finding out.

■ **Ask for only one thing at a time.** Don't dump a pile of requests on people. It will most likely turn them off. You wouldn't want to be saddled with a number of requests for aid so you shouldn't expect others to.

■ **Never ask directly for a job.** Networking provides a forum for people to seek advice, not jobs. If you're looking for a specific job, ask people what they like about their job and what advice they would give for someone interested in a similar position.

■ **Be willing to give as well as receive.** You must be willing to help others if you expect others to help you.

■ **Take notes when networking.** Immediately after the session record the pertinent facts of the encounter in a notebook or use a mini-tape recorder. I do. It speeds things up while networking. You can transcribe the information later to a permanent file.

■ **Keep files on all your network contacts and encounters.** I keep mine on a computer file for easy update. A computer isn't necessary, however, but what is important is the name, date, circumstances, and details of the encounter. For new contacts I include a short biography and personal appearance description so I'll remember who the person was. Don't neglect to include some personal asides about the individual. People are flattered when you remember little things said of a personal nature in past conversations. It shows you care and are interested in them.

■ **Follow up on leads.** Let those who gave you the leads know the results of your follow-up. People are gratified when their efforts result in helping others. Reporting back lets them know they didn't waste their time, and they will be glad to help you again.

Advice for Introverts

Not everyone is comfortable with the idea of networking. The very thought of approaching someone you don't know to ask advice strikes terror in the very soul of many. I know. I was one of those. I hung around the edges of parties and groups, not mingling, wishing the party was over so I could return to the security of my home. Meanwhile, my wife was carrying on a conversation with new acquaintances and having the time of her life, while I looked on with envy at her ability to start up new relationships.

She taught me a valuable lesson in dealing with new people. She told me to search for someone who, like myself, is hanging around the edges afraid to become involved. Approach that person with a big smile – a great conversation starter. Follow up by asking something about that person. All of us like to talk about things important and familiar to us. Above all, listen with interest. Follow the rules of good listening previously discussed. Such action guarantees success and frequently uncovers the most exciting people at the gathering, leading to new and long-lasting friendships.

Whatever your desire for retirement, networking can be your avenue for achievement. Networking has the dual advantage of information for your success and relationships for your psyche. What more could one ask?

Chapter Eight

Time:

The Retiree's

Most Precious Resource

A man who dares to waste one hour of time has not discovered the value of life – Charles Darwin (1809-1882)

The universal complaint of all retired people, once they begin an active, fulfilling retirement, is not having enough time to do all the things they want to do and need to get done. Many marvel that they now seem to have less time than before retirement. "When did I ever have time to work before I retired?" is a recurring theme.

Most retired people end up doing a number of diverse activities during retirement: volunteering, part-time work, home-business, consulting, the arts, travel, hobbies, and recreation activities. I've certainly found this to be true, and have used many of the time-planning methods of this chapter.

Time is our most important resource, and the older we get the more valuable it becomes. You and I are more aware than our younger brothers and sisters of its value. When we were younger, time seemed to stand still. I remember as a teenager believing I would never reach twenty-one. Time began to pick up speed, to go faster and faster the older I got. Time becomes more valuable when we have yet to accomplish those things still left undone. As we age we come to recognize the truth, that our own time is limited. Time lost is gone forever. Don't waste yours.

Good Time Management

Time management is nothing more than determining what is most important to you and then developing a plan to accomplish it. Not very mysterious, is it? You're right, it's pretty simple stuff. It makes you wonder why we don't do a better job of it. Part of the problem is that we let things distract us from our goals. Unless we formalize our efforts to keep our eye firmly on the target, we do a lot of wild shooting instead of hitting the bull's-eye.

Once your major retirement goals and subgoals have been defined, good daily time management gets them done. Daily time management is your plan of the day for doing all those things that are important to you without wasting time on those things that are not.

Did you catch the words "important to you"? This is the critical phrase in time management — those things important to you. We often spend enormous amounts of time doing things we care little about and then lament the fact that we don't have the time for the things we want to do most.

The proper use of time is a highly personal choice. What would seem frivolous to one may be exactly what is needed by another. Make your choices to fit your needs for yourself, not what others deem necessary. Of course you must consider satisfying joint responsibilities, but those should not completely foreshadow your own needs. Remember, you are important. Your needs come first.

Be Unavailable

Single-minded people who focus all their energy and concentration on one thing at a time seem to accomplish the most. Such single-mindedness prevents interruptions from keeping you from finishing. One way to avoid interruptions is to establish certain times you will be unavailable.

A writer friend, who works at home, was constantly being interrupted by friends wanting to talk on the phone. She solved this by passing the word that she would be unavailable from 7 A.M. to noon except for emergencies. To make it work, she screened all her calls through a telephone answering machine.

Time-Management Practices

Time-management experts cite four reasons why we fail to get the most from our available time:

★ We fail to set priorities on the things we need to do.

★ We lazily leave things undone, promising to do them some other time.

★ We often try to do more than is possible.

★ We waste too much time trying to do a perfect job.

Getting organized is the key to managing time effectively. The following guidelines will help you to get the things done that are important in your life.

■ **Develop a Plan.** Being busy won't get the job done. It's what you're busy at that counts. Be busy only with those things that are important to you. Managing your time means you work smarter, not harder. It gives you the control to accomplish what's most important and satisfying for you.

The control of your time begins by developing a plan. Your time-management program was given a major push if you set your major goals and subgoals after reading chapter 4. They provide the overall long-term strategy for your time-management program. Now you must integrate your goals into your daily schedule along with your other needs. You must also make allowances for both goals and leisure. A plan without room for leisure and other activities is doomed.

■ **Determine Priorities.** The orderly and logical achievement of long-term goals requires the setting of priorities. Priorities should become a part of your daily routine, a necessity to focus your effort toward your goals along with your other day-to-day needs and activities. Priorities should be set based on what is critical now, what can be left until later, and what can be ignored.

Alan Lakein, author of the classic time-management book, *How To Get Control of Your Time and Your Life,* advises using his A-B-C method of setting priorities. He advocates placing As on those items that are the most critical, Bs on the less critical, and Cs on items that can be left for a later time. Often the Cs lose their importance and are dropped. Once the priorities have been set you must work on all the As before Bs, and Bs before Cs. This means you are working on the important things instead of wasting effort on a task simply because it's easier or more readily accomplished.

■ **Scheduling.** Scheduling is setting aside the time for the things you want to do. Established routines help people get things done. Scheduling a certain time to do things and then sticking to it is a good way to apply your efforts where they'll do the most good.

We all have multiple interests, and a satisfying balanced retirement lifestyle demands we devote time to all the things that contribute to our well-being. Scheduling can help you accomplish that balance. Set aside a part of each day to do your important, high-priority work. Provide time each day for exercise to keep yourself fit. Pick an exercise activity you enjoy doing, something that gives you pleasure. Daily, my wife and I walk around our local park lake, a walk we look forward to each day with anticipation. Also, schedule time for other people and other activities. You must schedule for a balance of things that will both satisfy your goals and your other psychological needs.

Realize that a schedule is not something fixed in cement. You schedule to provide your wants, and as your wants change, so should your schedule.

■ **Set Deadlines.** Set deadlines for getting critical jobs done. Without deadlines jobs pile up to pressure you into stressful last-minute efforts or are left undone. Tackle your larger jobs step by step, each step with a deadline for completion. To eliminate the frustration of missed deadlines, make certain yours are set realistically.

■ **Break Jobs into Smaller Bites.** Most goals and subgoals can't be accomplished at a single sitting. Reduce them to smaller steps to become a part of your daily do-list. Breaking such jobs into workable segments allows you to put priorities on them and schedule them along with other daily tasks. This is the only effective way major goals can be attacked, to assure that you take action on them on a continuing basis.

■ **Seek Help.** Don't be afraid to ask for help or delegate tasks to others. Frequently someone else is better qualified to do the job. Hire outside help when the job needs experts or professionals. Doing so may turn out to be the best and least expensive way.

■ **Do the Hard Jobs During Your Best Hours.** Are you a morning person or a night person? Do your difficult jobs when you are at your mental and physical peak. We all differ when that occurs.

■ **A Place For Everything.** Much time may be wasted in finding things. The old adage, "A place for everything and everything in its place," is good advice. Know where your tools are. Keep your home office uncluttered, with records filed in some logical manner.

■ **Not Everything Is Manageable.** Recognize that some things cannot be scheduled, but must be viewed as a contingency. Know there will be interruptions by things that are unanticipated or unscheduled. Make room for these contingencies in any time plan or schedule.

■ **Don't Be Afraid To Say No.** Many overworked people can't say "no." While it is important to make yourself available to others, it is equally important to learn when you've done enough and finally say "No, I don't have the time for that." Frequently, your repeated help becomes viewed as your responsibility instead of the favor that was originally intended and thus is less appreciated.

■ **Be Satisfied, Not Perfect.** Don't waste time on being perfect in everything you do. Know when you've done enough and then go on to something else. A writer must eventually stop revising, a painter must eventually accept the picture as complete. Neither has reached perfection and never will but they must accept their own levels of satisfaction, and so must you.

■ **Don't Procrastinate.** One of our greatest failings is to say, "I'll do it later." Don't put off today's work to be done tomorrow, for tomorrow rarely comes. If it's important enough to do today, do it, otherwise forget it altogether. Keep on top of your personal and business mail by handling each piece of mail only once. Answer those letters that need answering, file those that need filing, and round file the rest. A quick trick for answering is to write your answer to questions on the same letter received. This speeds your reply and assures accuracy.

It's so easy to get in the habit of letting things slide. Once started, this becomes a habit. Many putter away their time on things that are not important to keep from doing the one thing that needs doing. Don't be a putterer. Get on with it.

Ginny Bindy, a seventy-seven-year-old retired nurse, knows how to get the most out of her day. Ginny is a volunteer at both the aquarium and the hospital. She also works part-time at a bakery, and still finds time to socialize with friends. Ginny "clocks" herself on repetitive jobs, and works at only those things important to her, a practice she's had since childhood.

"I just want to know how long things take without hurrying," she said. "It helps, knowing what jobs I have time for when things need doing."

Do-lists

Do-lists are effective tools used by successful busy people. Those who use them get the important things done, and still find time to enjoy other pursuits.

Do-lists work because they put organization into your life. The writing of the list reminds you of what is needed and what can be ignored. It's just as important to know what not to waste your time on as to know what needs to be done today. We all waste time on inconsequential tasks when we should be tackling those projects that need doing. A do-list helps eliminate such action.

There are two types of do-lists, master do-lists for attacking long-term projects and goals, and daily do-lists for doing what needs doing today. The two lists complement each other. The daily do-list integrates the master do-list items with today's "have-to's." The master do-list keeps your eye and your effort directed toward your major goals. Your daily do-list maintains your goal effort while getting the important daily tasks done.

Your do-lists are where your priorities and scheduling are applied. This is where you determine what's most important, less important, and what can be left undone for a later time or not at all. Remember the A-B-C method of setting priorities? Scheduling is as simple as numbering your high-priority items in order of necessity. Once determined, begin working with number one, followed by number two, etc.

I use do-lists. I maintained and monitored a master computerized do-list along with interview subjects for this book. My daily hand-written do-list included items from my master list.

Tickler Files

Tickler files are those handy little calendar files that spotlight important appointments, coming events, milestones, and due dates. What would we do without them?

A good calendar, with space for annotating notes, is all that is needed for your yearly tickler file. Yearly ticklers are marked on the calendar at the beginning of each year and updated as necessity demands throughout the year. Many of our important events, such as birthdays, anniversaries, reunions, and special events, repeat year after year. Other important happenings such as seminars and important meetings are added as required.

■ **Weekly/Monthly Ticklers.** A desk calendar in the form of a note pad is a handy device for jotting down daily and weekly reminders of coming events and items that need doing at certain times.

■ **Computerized Ticklers.** If you own a computer, it is a handy device for keeping a master tickler file or master do-list. Such files are easy to update and change as the need arises. It is especially valuable for maintaining a master do-list, providing an easy means for selecting items for your daily do-list.

Laural and Vince Maloney are avid do-list and tickler file users, something they learned and used extensively in their preretirement travel agency and real estate businesses. Now retired, they still rely on them to keep their busy retirement activities of property management, volunteer work, social obligations, and travel on track. Vince's do-list is a list of items numbered in the desired order to be accomplished. Laural uses both do-lists and tickler files. Her long-range tickler is a yearly calendar with room for daily comments, and she uses a desk note pad calendar for getting the daily/weekly have-to's done.

Harvest Those Inspirations

A micro-cassette pocket recorder is an excellent time-saving device for harvesting those flashes of inspiration that come to all of us. For example, in your search for the solution to some knotty problem, making your subconscious mind aware of the problem sets the forces in action for future flashes of insight. Be prepared when they come with a way to record them so they won't be lost. If you don't have a recorder, carry a pencil and pocket notebook wherever you go. Don't leave home without them. I use a pocket recorder and get some of my best writing ideas and solutions while traveling in the car or taking my morning walk. I find it's my most valuable crutch.

We all are faced with those cracks, crevices, and dead spots of time that creep into our day. Don't let waiting in line or in waiting rooms and doctor's offices upset you. Use the time to your advantage. Catch up on some important reading or that new novel you've been wanting to start. Write a letter to a friend. Work on the solution to some problem. Use a Walkman to learn all types of subjects via audio cassette tapes.

Traveling and driving a car present opportunities to utilize the many training or learning audio cassettes available, or to listen to a story or book that has been recorded on cassette. Practically every area of interest has been recorded, opening up possibilities to learn almost anything by cassette. Don't overlook the relaxation of just enjoying the ride with some of your favorite music for company.

Make your wait an advantage instead of an aggravation. Think of it as an opportunity.

Good time management stems from organizing and planning time for what is most important to you. Apply the above procedures for accomplishing your retirement goals. But don't forget to include room for leisure and recreation – things like searching the sky for images in the clouds, and other endeavors that promote good health, happiness, and well-being.

Chapter Nine

Resumes:

Write Your Own

Advertisement

I am the master of my fate; I am the captain of my soul. – William E. Henley (1849-1903)

Not every retired career seeker needs a resume. Some of you may get what you want through your personal network, bypassing the need for one. However, if you do need a resume, you need one that works for you, not against you, one that presents you in the best possible terms.

When was the last time you needed a resume? Some number of years ago, I would wager – or maybe never. Perhaps you spent your work life climbing the same career ladder, or you were a home-maker without a formal career. In either case, you may need one now. One of the first things human services people want to see is a written description of your skills and qualifications. That means relearning the forgotten skill of resume writing.

Some career consultants malign the resume. They consider it to be outdated, no longer a viable tool. Some say you should replace it with a qualification brief or an outline of your qualifications in a letter. Nonsense. A rose is a rose, and by any other name, a resume is still a resume, one of the job market's major requirements.

There are compelling reasons for you to write your own resume. Doing so forces you to examine all of your skills, qualifications, and accomplishments pertinent to the job. This is especially important if you are transferring skills from one career area to another. Writing your own resume builds confidence and self-worth by focusing your attention on just what an accomplished and valuable person you are. Also, the self-evaluation required to write your resume helps prepare you for that all-important interview. And by writing your own resume, you can avoid the often recognizable, cliched verbiage of a professional resume writer.

If you are entering the job market for the first time or after a long absence, you may be suffering from low self-esteem and lack of confidence. It is important that you feel good about yourself, because it is difficult to sell yourself to others until you yourself are sold. That is what writing your own resume can do for you. A good resume builds confidence and self-esteem. A good resume advertises you to the job market in the best, most positive way possible to help you sell yourself.

Homemakers often are unaware of their true value to the job market. Many fail to recognize the skills and experiences gained through homemaking and volunteering, mistakenly believing the only skills with value are those involving paid work. All homemakers reentering the job market will find valuable assistance in defining their skills by reading *The Women's Job Search Handbook* by Bloomberg and Holden and *Have Skills Women's Workbook: Finding jobs using your homemaking and volunteer work experience* by Ruth B. Ekstrom.

Elizabeth Verona had always been a homemaker. When her husband retired, his pension was enough for the two of them. But when he died, the part of his pension left for her reduced her income to the poverty level, forcing her to seek work. Having never held a job outside her home, Elizabeth believed she was unqualified for any position. Then she began writing her resume for a part-time assistant librarian's position and found her love for books and previous experience as a volunteer public school librarian qualified her for the position. Writing her resume made her aware of her qualifications and gave her the confidence to be a success during the interview. She got the part-time job, which eventually became full-time.

I remember my first resume. It had a line or two about my education, then it listed my jobs and duties in chronological order, and ended with the names and addresses of several references. But times have changed and so have resumes.

Modern resumes are no longer the classic, dull litanies of past jobs. Today they are directed to the job being applied for and they are positive, functional descriptions of skills, qualifications, and achievements important to the specific position being sought. An effective resume advertises you honestly to the job market in terms important to prospective employers. And the resume must be directed toward a specific job objective. Generalized resumes are ineffective. Therefore you must write different resumes to satisfy different job objectives.

Were you to research the library for resume advice, you would find enough paper generated on the subject to blot dry a sizable body of water. Much that has been written is obsolete and contradictory due to changing times. This has resulted in many outdated, ineffective resumes. Perhaps that is why some job counselors have a negative attitude toward resumes.

The jobs go to those who can sell themselves most effectively. And selling yourself is what we are talking about, a fact that many resume authors fail to understand. You are best served by modeling your resume after the world of sales and advertising.

Use Advertising Techniques

■ **The Headline.** Advertising experts agree that the headline is the single most important part of the ad. The headline is the grabber. It is the lead-in to entice the customer to read on. A good headline tells the whole story – what's being offered and how the customer will benefit. A good headline is the focal point for all the supporting copy to focus on. Without an effective headline, the ad's main body copy may never get read. Or, in your case, the resume may end up in the round file.

■ **Job Objective Statement.** Your job objective statement is the headline – the single most important statement in your resume. It is impossible to write an effective resume until you have clearly defined and stated your job objective because everything in the resume must support that objective. An effective job objective statement presents your objective and highlights your skills and attributes of greatest benefit to those who hire.

Think of yourself as a product for sale to perform the job you want. Determine what benefits you bring to the job. Such analysis leads to the development of a successful job objective statement.

Good Job Objective Statements

Look at the following job objective statements. See how the objectives state specific abilities and relate those abilities to an employer's needs.

OBJECTIVE: A programming position requiring in-depth knowledge of hardware circuit logic; real-time operating systems design; and language proficiencies in Assembler, Basic, Fortran, and Cobol.

OBJECTIVE: A responsible position in financial management with a firm where my office management skills, organizational ability, and familiarity with computerized financial systems would be an asset.

OBJECTIVE: A position of responsibility in the accounting field where years of experience are valued and solutions to uncommon accounting problems are welcomed.

OBJECTIVE: A job working for a contractor who desires a full range of remodeling and cabinet-making skills.

OBJECTIVE: Office manager or sales manager for an organization needing my ability and enthusiasm to motivate people to excel.

OBJECTIVE: A position designing and planning telecommunication networks, where innovative yet cost-effective systems are desired.

OBJECTIVE: Property management of an apartment/town house complex of less than thirty units, where a proven ability to lower owner costs and maintain good tenant rapport is desirable.

OBJECTIVE: A machinist position requiring job-shop skills, operating a diverse variety of manually or numerically controlled machine tools.

OBJECTIVE: Activity director or counselor for young adults or seniors, where my empathy and advisory skill would be valuable.

OBJECTIVE: A position in facility maintenance leading to maintenance management for an organization desiring an improved facility maintained by a master craftsman who enjoys his work.

These job objective statements are all different yet they all have three things in common: Each clearly defines the position desired, each focuses on outstanding skills or attributes, and each presents the skills in ways important to an employer.

Body Copy

Let's go back to the advertising experts and look to the support copy, the copy that supports the headline – your job objective statement. This copy is called body copy in advertising. Proper body copy presents the promise of the headline benefit by benefit, each benefit ranked in order of importance from the most important to the least important.

Successful copy goes straight to the point. What is said is far more important than how it is said. Good copy statements are direct and precise, promoting acceptance, whereas broad, vague copy statements cause skepticism. Make copy credible through your achievements. Good copy avoids superlatives and is written for a sixth grade level audience. The highly educated are never offended by simple, clear English. And above all, good copy is truthful.

NAME

ADDRESS, ZIP CODE   PHONE NUMBER

OBJECTIVE: Managing and Supervising Software Development where superior planning, coordinating, analyzing and communicating skills are important.

EXPERIENCE

MANAGING/SUPERVISING

My data processing career has been a staircase of increased levels of responsibility from a project leader directing programming efforts to a department head managing project supervisors in developing complex ADP projects.

- Major achievement: Received Superior Accomplishment Award in form of quality salary increase and Letter of Commendation for managing installation of complex ADP systems into two satellite organizations.
- Department head over ADP Planning and Analysis.
- Supervised ten programmers and systems analysts.
- Managed the design and implementation of software.
- Managed conversion of software from one computer to another.

COORDINATING/PLANNING/ANALYZING

Practiced and developed my coordinating and analyzing skills throughout my entire work history.

- Coordinated implementation of Large Scale Computer.
- Coordinated DPD operations with programmers and users.
- Acted as liaison between vendors and management.
- Conducted computer capacity and software efficiency studies.

- Analyzed/improved work processes and material flow.
- Planned and conducted surveys; set work standards.
- Planned lesson plans and view graphs for group presentations.

COMMUNICATING/TRAINING

Excellent communicator. Thoroughly experienced in group presentations to audiences of varying backgrounds.

- Consultant representing local command to Chief of Naval Operations.
- Conducted meetings with peers and subordinates.
- Made numerous presentations to managers and others.
- Trained people in newly implemented hardware and software.
- Instructed 24 classes in use of ignition analyzer.
- Wrote procedures and issued directives.
- Wrote free-lance articles, sailing handbook, and job resumes.
- Lectured at job-finding seminar; interviewed resume clients.

WORK HISTORY

Job title, company name, location, years employed, followed by each job in descending order.

EDUCATION

Highest college degree, college name, state, and awards. List lesser educational accomplishment in descending order.

OTHER FACTS: Something for them to remember you by – something important to an employer.

The Resume Copy

Let's dissect the sample resume. See how the job objective state-ment promises are supported by the text. Notice how the body copy is divided into the three areas of promises spoken to in the job objective statement, with the most important promise described first.

The first promise, managing/supervising, focuses on the Managing and Supervising Software Development part of the job objective statement. See how the management and supervision skills have been specifically stated, " ... from a project leader directing pro-gramming efforts to a department head managing project supervi-sors in developing complex ADP projects."

Credibility is provided by the major achievement of a Quality Salary Award and of letters of commendation for managing the installation of complex ADP systems into two satellite organizations. Further evidence of management experience is bulleted in descending order of importance.

The second promise, coordinating/planning/analyzing, is directed toward the " ... where superior planning, coordinating, analyzing skills are important" portion of the job objective statement. The statement, "Practiced and developed my coordinating and ana-lyzing skills throughout my entire work history," indicates a pro-longed history of those skills backed up by representative bulleted examples.

The third and last promise, communicating/training, targets the " ... where superior communication skills are important" section of the job objective statement. A diversity of oral and written communi-cation experiences across a wide range of audiences, from trainees to the Chief of Naval Operations, is convincing evidence in support of communication skills.

If You're Overqualified

The subtle discrimination against the older and overqualified job seeker is still assiduously practiced in many areas. It's a strange fact that corporations shy away from hiring older or overqualified workers, yet actively seek them when using temporary help services or part-time help. They forgo costlier older, experienced workers for the less expensive younger employees to fill in-house positions, but prefer the older worker's skills and experience when temporary or part-time help is required.

Your awareness of this determines how you handle your resume. If seeking a career with temporary help services or volunteer organizations, let it all hang out as far as age or overqualification is concerned, because temps and volunteer groups and their clients actively seek retirees. By contrast, if applying for a job in the corporate world, it's best to mask your age and overqualification in the resume. Address it later during the interview, where the discrimination may be countered by a personable performance. People hire those they feel good about. It's up to you to make them feel good about you in the interview.

The 40-Plus members have found the best way to counter age discrimination on the resume is to tailor their resumes to reflect skills and accomplishments functionally. A functional format masks the age where possible. Additionally, some early work histories may also be left off, and education is usually described in college degrees received minus the dates.

Job-seekers at 40-Plus maintain their work-related experience, skills, and accomplishments on a PC computer data base. They construct a resume specifically tailored to whatever job or interview they are currently seeking. Such tailoring masks overqualification.

Emphasize Personal Achievements

Emphasize success through personal achievements, and verify successes through words of praise for jobs well done. Sell what you can do, not what you are.

Point to your accomplishments, those things that saved the company money, increased production, improved operations, or improved the work environment. Give examples of cost savings in dollars or improvement in percentages of change. Often percentage change is a more dramatic indicator than dollars. Also, salary increases by percentage will not disclose your previous salary.

Achievements are not always measurable in terms of savings, but may point to a superior knowledge or skill. Often your past successes may have been given oral praise by those you have worked for. Don't be afraid to use those comments to show success on the job.

Keep It Positive

Throughout your resume, as with Johnny Mercer's hit song of the forties, you must "accentuate the positive and eliminate the negative." Never, never lie in a resume, but never volunteer negative, damaging information either. Instead, present your best profile for the world to view.

Often personal information such as age and marital status may be considered negative by some and not by others. For that reason leave your personal data for the interview. By that time your skills and outstanding attitude will overshadow any negative aspects. In any case, you will have a better opportunity to counter any concerns, thus perhaps turning a negative into a positive.

Keep It Short and Tantalizing

Employers are busy people. They may have dozens of resumes to review in the quest for persons to be interviewed. Long, wordy resumes usually end up in the round file. Don't let that happen to you. Keep your resume in the active file by whetting the appetite of the reader with punchy statements directly to the point, focusing attention on your skills and giving them credibility through your accomplishments.

You don't have to tell it all. Leave something for the interview. A good rule is to keep your resume to a single page. If that's impossible, reserve the second page for secondary, backup data. Put all the essential information that tells your story on page one.

Keeping it to a single page is easier than you might think. One of the devices for doing so is to use simple, active sentences beginning with an action verb. Remember the manner in which you developed your activities list in chapter 3? The technique is the same. In fact, you will be using your activities list, as you will see later on. Your descriptions must cover only those items that will support your job objective statement. Everything else is superfluous and should be left out. Don't oversell the facts. Tell just enough to convey your skills and accomplishments, tantalizing the reader to want to hear more in an interview.

Give Your Resume Eye Appeal

A resume must be appealing to the eye to capture attention. A messy, sloppy, or poorly formatted resume may be discarded without being read. Obviously, your resume requires proper grammar, spelling, punctuation, and typing, but it also should be pleasing to the eye and demand the attention of the reader. Remember, your resume is a picture of you. You'll want your resume to stand out, to convey a favorable first impression and gain you an interview. Here are a few general guidelines for eye appeal:

★ Use short paragraphs with double spacing between.

- ★ Maintain large margins all around.
- ★ Generally use capital letters or boldface for headings and description titles.
- ★ Titles to the left of the text, or centered titles have eye appeal.
- ★ Underline, star, or bullet important information.
- ★ Use all of the paper with lots of intervening white space.
- ★ Try mixing formats.

Chronological or Functional?

Should your resume be chronologically or functionally presented? In most cases a functional sequence is superior. It presents your skills and accomplishments in the order of importance according to the job objective statement, which usually is not the order in which they were acquired through experience.

This is especially true for retiree career changers who want to transfer skills from an old career to a new one. Be aware that you have the advantage of a rich history of varied experiences to draw upon, many unrelated to your past career. Skills are skills no matter how they were gained and many are transferable, as you found out in chapter 3. Also, a functional presentation provides a means of summarizing and expanding on important skills and accomplishments rather than dutifully and dully repeating them throughout each work experience.

Although functional sequence is generally preferred, there is an exception. The exception is when the order of importance of the skills and accomplishments for the job objective statement and the order in which they were acquired coincide. When this occurs, a chronologically presented resume is a very powerful and effective advertisement of your skills.

Work History

Whether functional or chronological, the work history need give only the job title, name of the company, city, state, and dates of employment. All other job-related information is described functionally with your most important skills and accomplishments presented in the order of importance to satisfy the job objective statement. Some early jobs may best be left off, as previously indicated.

Dates — How Precise?

What you did is far more important than when you did it. Present dates as years only. How dates are handled depends upon how the resume is to be used, as previously discussed under age discrimination.

Education — What and Where?

Where does education go? That depends on its importance to the job objective statement. If you are a CPA, engineer, or in any profession in which educational credentials are important, the education listing should be at the beginning. This is also true for people who have had little or no work experience. On the other hand, once the bulk of your skills and accomplishments stems from job experience, education becomes less important and should be presented near the end.

State your education in positive terms. If you had three years of college but didn't get a degree, state the major, the college, and dates attended. Here, again, dates depend upon resume usage.

List the highest level of educational achievement first, followed in descending order by lesser degrees. Don't bother to include high school if you have a college degree. Include any academic accomplishments such as honor societies, academic awards, or other special achievements, for example, "graduated in top 3 percent of class" or "maintained 3.8 grade point average." All education directly

applicable to the job objective should be included, such as appren-
ticeships, military training, and self-help courses. Training not in
support of your objective should be left out.

Give Them a Finale

Keep them clapping! End your resume with pizazz, not with a
"ho-hum." Leave them something to remember you by. An excellent way to do so is to finish it under the title "Other Facts" or some
similar title, where you can reinforce some desirable attribute
previously stated or bring out new, interesting facts. Possibilities
include such things as published articles, professional memberships,
qualifying licenses, or personal attributes desirable in the work
place.

Putting It All Together

Now that you know what a good resume is, let's put yours together.
You've already started the first step by defining your job objective.
However, your job objective statement requires the addition of your
major skills to be complete. That is, you must include the several
major skill groups that will be expanded on in the body copy.

An easy way to do this is to go back to your chapter 3 activity list.
Carefully review your list, selecting all of the activity statements that
will support the job objective. Now, analyze those selected in the
light of the skills involved and arrange them into logical skill groupings.
To show you how this is done, we'll build a hypothetical resume
based on the following activity list.

ACTIVITIES LIST

Activity	Skill or attribute
C– Wrote how-to articles, resumes & classified ads	writing

C–	Wrote sailing handbook	writing
C–	Issued directives	writing
C–	Wrote procedures	writing
C–	Interviewed resume clients and sailors for handbook	interviewing
B–	Analyzed interview data for resumes	analyzing
B–	Organized resume data	organizing
C–	Lectured job-finding seminar	public speaking
B–	Researched writing assignment (sailing and job-finding)	researching
	Designed/developed diving equipment (manufactured, sold equipment)	creative development
	Designed/developed toys (for toy manufacturer)	creative development
	Machined small plastic/metal parts for development	machining
	Build/machine one-time items for own pleasure	working with hands
	Repetitive production of diving equipment	repetitive production
A–	Supervised ten people, planning/analysis in ADP	supervision
A–	Department head of planning/analysis in ADP	supervised other managers
C–	Trained numerous people implementing hardware/software	teaching
C–	Instructed 24 classes in ignition analysis	teaching
B–	Planned lesson plans for training/presentations	planning
B–	Developed viewgraphs for presentations	planning
C–	Made numerous presentations to managers and others	public speaking
C–	Conducted meetings with peer/subordinates	communications
A–	Developed computer programs as a project leader	supervising

C–	Consultant representing local command to Chief of Naval Operations	consultant
B–	Coordinated implementation of large-scale computer	coordinating
B–	Coordinated DPD operations with programmers and users	coordinating
A–	Managed installation of ADP at Lemoore/ Moffett	managing
A–	Managed design and implementation of software	managing
A–	Managed conversion of software from one ADP to another	managing
B–	Conducted ADP capacity studies and software efficiency studies	analyzing
B–	Liaison between vendors and management	liaison
B–	Analyzed/improved work processes & material flow	analyzing
B–	Conduct surveys/establish work standards	analyzing
A–	Received superior accomplishment award via quality salary increase, and letter of commendation for managing installation of complex ADP systems into two satellite organizations.	management achievement

The Job Objective Statement

Let's assume the basic job objective is "Software Development Manager." From the activity list, select each activity on the list that will support managing software development. Next, group similar skills. Our knowledge of the basic objective helps us determine what the skill groupings and relative order of importance should be. In this example, the groupings and order of importance are:

A. Managing/Supervising

B. Coordinating/Planning/Analyzing

C. Communicating/Training

The activities list illustrates how the major skill groups are keyed to the activity list entries, which later become the support text in the body copy.

We are now ready to finalize the job objective statement by merging the skill groups with the initial job objective. The result is as follows:

OBJECTIVE: Managing and supervising software development where superior planning, coordinating, analyzing, and communicating skills are important.

The result is a headline that defines the job objective in ways valuable to an employer and that will be supported fully by the body copy in the order of importance to job success. We have made a complete promise in the headline, a promise we will expand upon and substantiate in the supporting text of the body copy.

Building the Body Copy

By this time it must be clear that an activity list is essential in developing a good resume. A good activity list states each acquired activity in straightforward statements, usually beginning with an action verb. These become the nucleus for the copy.

In our example, we have identified the activities that supported the objective, and we have keyed each to its skill group. Now we must arrange the activities into priority sequence within their groups; we must combine similar statements where possible and then review what has been written to make it the best we can do. The review is best done after the writing is finished and has been put aside for a period of time. Only then will we be able to view our work with the detachment of an employer.

An effective way to start each skill group section is with a mini-heading: a statement that captures the gist of the copy describing that particular group. In our example we shall analyze the managing-

/supervising skill group. A study of the activities list entries coded with an "A," reveals a progression of management and supervising responsibilities from project leader to department head. This fact makes a fine mini-headline for the group in question and thus is stated as follows:

"My data processing career has been a staircase of increased levels of responsibility from a project leader directing program-ming efforts to a department head managing project supervisors in developing complex ADP projects."

The mini-headline is then followed by all of the management and supervision activity listing entries presented in priority sequence.

Each of the skill groups is analyzed and presented in a similar manner. The resume is a completed example of our case. Study this example carefully, comparing and analyzing it against the activities list to see how it was done.

Now you know how to write a resume that will sell you for the job you want. Don't just sit there! Get cracking!

Chapter Ten

Interviews:
Your Final Frontier

To be vanquished and yet not surrender, that is victory. — Jozef Pilsudski (1867-1935)

This is a tutorial designed to help those who have never been interviewed before and those who are experienced in interviewing. Each group faces unique problems and both share problems in common. Even if you are referred to a position by your personal network, you will most likely be interviewed before being accepted.

Many reach retirement without being interviewed for a job, and for others it was so long ago it holds little value now. Perhaps you never held a formal job before, but now that your spouse has died, you find yourself in need of work to supplement the reduced retirement annuity, or perhaps you've been working for the same company most of your adult life and haven't been interviewed since the beginning of your career.

As a professional, you may be well acquainted with the interview process, but now find yourself seeking a career in a field some consider you are overqualified or too old for. What do you do? How do you overcome those obstacles?

Regardless of whether this is your first time or one of many, being interviewed is a frightening experience. It doesn't matter whether you are a professional or a first-time job seeker, when rejection is a possibility, we all tremble. Even the most glib among us is concerned when being interviewed and our future is at stake. Why? Because the control rests in the hands of the interviewer. Those who say they are unconcerned are likely to fare poorly.

Two Types of Interviews

You will probably encounter two general types of placement interviews, the screening interview and the selection interview. The personnel departments of large companies usually conduct screening interviews, talking with a large number of applicants to find the most promising candidates. This interview concentrates on applicable work experience, education, and training to determine who is qualified enough for further consideration. The selection interview determines who gets the job. It is conducted by the person you'll be working for if you get the job. You want to impress this person with your accomplishments and your ability to work in harmony with him or her. Persons conducting selection interviews are looking for more than just a qualified candidate; they want someone with whom they can feel comfortable while working.

The company's purpose for the interview is to hire for a position; your purpose for the interview is to receive a job offer. Keep those goals firmly in your mind. Remember: You are dealing with managers trying to fill a position that needs filling, not hiring experts. They are managers first and hiring officials only by necessity. And don't forget that this is a selling game. They are the buyers; you are the seller. They desperately want to buy, and your job is to help them make a decision to buy you by making you an offer.

Your Goals in Interviews

Your first goal during the interview is to determine if the position is right for you. If it is, your next goal is to project the image that you are the person the company needs and wants to hire.

A third possible goal is to have the company create a job around your unique talents. It is not unusual for an outstanding interview performance to result in the offer of an entirely different job, one created for your special mix of skills.

Pleasing the Interviewer

A 1989 survey of 625 California business executives conducted by the Thomas Temporaries, a temporary help service headquartered in Irvine, California, found specific characteristics that helped or hindered applicants for jobs. Here they are:

Turn-offs: bad first impression, arrogance, pushy attitude, interrupting, talking too much, evasiveness, lack of confidence, lack of job skills.

Turn-ons: good first impression, confidence, enthusiasm, sincerity, honesty, good communication skills, pleasing personality, applicable job skills.

The company believes that if you have troubles in these areas, work on the following: Create a good first impression with eye contact, good posture, a firm handshake, and appropriate attire. Be friendly, be enthusiastic, be honest, and be yourself. Listen and provide clear, thoughtful answers. Ask intelligent questions. Know the company and what skills you have that are valuable to the position. Write a note of thanks following the interview.

First Impression

Interviewers are impressed by a good appearance, a pleasing personality, enthusiasm, motivation, and communication skills. Your command of speech gives them a measure of your intelligence and competence. Obviously, you need the skills to do the job, but often that becomes less important to the interviewer than those items just named.

People make judgments based on what you appear to be, not what you are. The impression you make is far more important than your actual credentials. First impressions are the ones that linger the longest and have the greatest effect on the outcome of the interview. The interviewer, who may be your future boss, is interested in working with someone who fits in, someone he or she feels good about, someone who can be trusted to get the job done.

Your first impression must give interviewers a good positive feeling about you. Project a vigorous, energetic image. Direct eye contact and a firm handshake greeting are a must. Tell them how pleased you are at the prospect of working in such a position.

Many younger managers fear older employees will cling to old ideas and methods, and resist learning and applying new techniques. Indicate your openness to new ideas and challenges.

Age Discrimination

Despite the laws to the contrary, all mature job seekers face the problem of age discrimination. If your resume was designed to your advantage, the age issue may not have come up until you walk in the door and the interviewer sees you for the first time. Despite the initial surprise felt by the interviewer, waiting until the interview to address the age problem is in your favor. If your age had been known earlier you might not have gotten the interview. In any case, the interview gives you the best opportunity to counter the age objection. Emphasize positive aspects of your age: Work ethic, loyalty, good health, energy, enthusiasm, maturity, flexibility, and willingness to take responsibility.

Express the experience and maturity you bring to the position but emphasize your willingness to embrace new ideas. You might say, "If experience has taught me anything, it has brought home the fact that times and conditions change, and we must change with them if we are to succeed."

Let them know you don't mind working for someone younger, because you believe age is not a criteria for leadership, and you feel comfortable learning from others, regardless of their age.

Point out that you, as a retiree, may represent a valuable asset to the company in the form of someone willing to work odd shifts or holidays and weekends, or perhaps part-time to take up the slack. Frequently retired people prefer not to compete with weekend and holiday crowds for parks and recreation areas, reserving uncrowded weekdays to enjoy those areas.

Overqualified?

If you have a rich career background and seek a position of considerably lesser responsibility, you face the problem of being overqualified.

If you wrote your resume properly, identifying only the information necessary to support the position, perhaps the interviewer will not be aware of your overqualification. On the other hand, if you were referred to the position by a friend or colleague, the truth is out. In either case it may become obvious during the interview.

The best way to counter the overqualification problem is to describe your retirement career motives for seeking the position, which are entirely different from those of your wage-earning career days. Explain why the position is important to you with those new needs in mind. Be careful not to position your stated retirement needs in conflict with the employer's needs and goals.

Age discrimination and overqualification usually are not problems when you seek work for small businesses. They are more concerned about your ability to do the job and less concerned about your age or what you did before. Two other areas free from age and overqualification discrimination are the temporary help services and volunteer organizations. Both prefer retirees.

Retired professionals could be seen as a threat to the interviewer due to their experience and past track record. They should play down their accomplishments. If you're in this position, acknowledge a desire to involve yourself in what's new in the profession, and what younger professionals like the interviewer can contribute to your knowledge in a changing field.

Know the Company

Before going to an interview, you should find out all you can about the company and the job being offered. Talk to people who work for the company and who work for similar companies doing similar jobs. Study company literature, financial statements, newspaper articles, trade journals, and any other sources you can find. Find out, if you can, what's bugging the bosses. It need not be a big thing. It might be some small concern connected with the job such as wanting someone who is dependable by always being on time and rarely ill, or someone who is willing to work odd hours and frequently work overtime.

Learn all about the position being offered and the person interviewing you. The more you know the easier it is for you to appeal to the company's and interviewer's self-interests. Don't forget for a moment that this is a selling game. They are the buyers and you are the seller. To be a successful salesperson you must know your clients, know what emotional buttons turn them on, and what will make them want to hire you.

Your Strengths and Weaknesses

The interview is the place to give life to your resume, to expand upon it, and to give it credence. If you've written your resume following the suggestions outlined in chapter nine, it has set the stage by briefly spelling out those factors important to the job and leaving out those that are not.

Be prepared to counter anything that could be construed as negative. Analyze your problem areas in the light of the position. Pick out the two or three weakest parts of your resume in relation to the job, and prepare as positive a response as possible.

Analyze your achievements, especially those that indicate abilities valuable to the job for which you're being interviewed. Examine the skills and problem-solving you've done in the past. Are they applicable here? If so, be prepared to let the interviewer know about them. Describe them when you are asked, "What skills do you bring to the job?" or "What qualifies you for this position?" or "Tell me about yourself."

The salary discussion shouldn't surface until near the end of the interview. Let the interviewer broach the subject. When asked, instead of giving a specific figure, respond with a salary range based on your research. Prepare for this by reviewing the salaries of people who work in the same or similar positions, querying other employees, and checking with trade and professional associations. If you are more interested in the position than the salary, say that job satisfaction is your primary goal, and the salary is secondary.

During the interview, don't be afraid to ask questions. Use a questioning and listening technique to help you zero in on what their needs and problems are. Ask specific open-ended questions, well thought out in advance, questions beginning with what, why, or how and that require detailed responses that keep the dialogue open. While you're listening you can't talk yourself out of the job, and the interviewer can't say no while answering questions.

Two good questions to ask are "What do you feel is the most important qualification for the position?" and "What are some of the problems you would like solved?"

Asking questions about the job shows your interest, and their answers to your questions provide an opportunity for you to show how your skills and abilities provide solutions for their needs.

Have Your Answers Ready

■ **"Tell me about yourself."** Be careful with this one. Use this opportunity to talk about your skills and accomplishments that are related to the position. Don't crow about achievements and skills that show your overqualification, if that is the case.

■ **"Why do you want to work here?"** Your answer should be in terms of a benefit to the company, not just that you want something to do or you want to make a little extra money. They're interested in hiring people who are interested in the company and the type of service or product they provide.

■ **"What do you consider your greatest strength?"** This is your opportunity to show off your skills for the position backed up with some accomplishment that provides credibility.

■ **"What do you consider your greatest weakness?"** Everyone has weaknesses. If possible, make your weakness a plus by describing one that is a valuable attribute for the position. As an example, if the job requires a team player, then a weakness that you like to bounce ideas off others would be an advantage. By contrast, if the job required unassisted research, the weakness of being a loner who prefers to work in isolation would be an advantage.

■ **"What did you like most and least about past jobs?"** Tell them about those things you did and enjoyed that are important to the present position; describe those things you disliked that are unimportant to the present job.

■ **"What makes you qualified for this position?"** Here's another opportunity to expound upon your skills and accomplishments important to this job.

■ **"Why are you interested in a job you are obviously overqualified for?"** Your interests have changed and you no longer seek the stress of the prior career. Also, money is no longer the primary consideration. Stress those transferable skills and attributes you now wish to use in a new and different career, one that offers new experiences and provides a balance for your new lifestyle.

Mel Macon, a retired retail manager for one of the nation's largest department store chains, applied for an entry level retail clerk position in a gift shop. The interviewer was concerned about Mel's obvious overqualification for the position. Mel assured him that he was no longer interested in the stress of management, and that one of the things that had originally attracted him to retail sales was the interaction with the public, something he missed and wanted to get back to. Now that he was retired he felt he could afford to work at those things he enjoyed the most, unconcerned about scrambling up the career ladder. He also indicated a desire to work part-time and odd hours, a fact beneficial to both. He got the job.

Closing for the Job

Any good salesperson will tell you one of the most important aspects of the sales pitch is asking for the sale. That's exactly what you must do – ask for the position. As the interview begins to run down, after all the questions have been asked and answered, ask for the position by posing the following questions:

"Do you think I can do the job?"

The interviewers can answer in only two ways, with either a yes or a no. If they say no, you should ask: "Where do you think I'm light?"

Their explanation will reopen the dialogue for you to clarify any skills or abilities that show you are qualified, if in fact you are. If you truly lack the necessary qualifications, at least it provides knowledge of what skills you must improve to become so.

If they say yes, they feel you can do the job, you should ask: "Are you going to make me an offer?"

Try to shoot for a solid yes or no, not a wishy-washy maybe. A maybe is frequently a copout for a polite no. If you can't get a definite answer, press for a specific date for the final decision. If the answer is no, find out why for future interviews. If the answer is yes, you've won – now find out what the next step is.

Remember that they want to hire someone, and asking for their position often is the nudge that pushes them in your direction.

Never end an interview without closing for the position.

Role-Playing

If you haven't been interviewed before, or are concerned about your performance, I recommend you role-play the interview with a friend or family member. Role-playing requires researching and anticipating the type of questions you will be asked in the interview and then setting up an interview to play out the roles. Your friend or relative acts as the interviewer and of course you are cast in the role of the person being interviewed.

The roles should be played out all the way, including your arrival and initial greeting, followed by all the questions and interactions you are likely to encounter. End with your closing for the sale.

You need to evaluate your progress and highlight those areas that need improvement. One way is to use a tape recorder. A playback of the results for critical review is a great aid in highlighting your weaknesses. Hearing your own voice and the way you respond can be a real education.

An even better tool is to videotape the pretend interview. This has the added benefit of viewing your appearance and visual responses, a most important consideration since these are so important. If you don't own a video camera or have a friend who does, check your local Yellow Pages for video rentals.

Get a third person to witness the proceedings. This will add critical advice on how to improve your interview performance. Pay particular attention to your voice pitch and quality. Was it strong and confident? Did you speak clearly and intelligently?

If you used a video, review the manner in which you greeted the interviewer, your body language, and posture. Were your clothing and appearance suitable? Did you project energy and enthusiasm? Did you look the interviewer directly in the eye? Did your facial expression and body attitude project a good impression?

Does video role-playing work? Yes, even the seasoned professionals at 40-Plus use video cameras for mock interviews. They are critiqued by other members who are experts in the fields being interviewed. It works for them and it will work for you.

Be patient and know that success is built by learning from your failures. Everyone fails but only those who profit from their failures succeed. Don't think of an unsuccessful interview as a failure but rather as a learning experience. Analyze each unsuccessful interview. That will help you to gain that future success.

Make your interview a success. Know yourself. Be yourself. And sell yourself.

Chapter Eleven

Temporary or
Part-time Work

Without work all life goes rotten. – Albert Camus (1913-1960)

Temporary help services (temps) can be your best avenue to a retirement career. Today's temps are all things to all career seekers, and there is no age discrimination. In fact, many companies prefer and ask for older temporary employees.

Many Services

The temporary help service industry is no longer just the purveyor of traditional office help, supplying a narrow array of clerks and typists. It now covers a full spectrum of services to the work world. Through specialization, all professions and technical careers are included in today's temporary help industry. Specialization represents the fastest growing segment of the industry.

It's a very diverse industry. It blankets most career areas, everything from the singing telegram to designing buildings. Temporary help services offer the retiree the greatest opportunities and flexibility, and the largest number of job choices for reentering the work force. They provide a broad range of professional, technical, and industrial services. There are more than 7,800 help services nationwide.

The San Francisco Telephone Yellow Pages lists 107 different temps, offering eighty-seven types of functions. Some of the functional areas embrace a number of different careers and disciplines. As an example, accounting may include CPAs, financial managers, financial analysts, senior accountants, tax consultants, and auditors. One agency listed twenty-one unusual temporary services including clowns, a breakfast-in-bed service, Santas, and live-ins for those who need constant help and companionship. Its motto is "Name it and we probably already provide it."

Temporary workers fall into three broad classes of work, lower-skilled repetitive work, high-tech clerical and technical skills, and executives and professionals. The industry itself encompasses four major occupational areas: office and clerical, industrial, technical and professional, and medical.

Don't confuse temporary help services with employment agencies. Temps hire part-time help and assume the obligations of the employer. When you sign on with a temp, you're under its direction and control in an employer and employee relationship. It recruits, hires, and makes work assignments to companies based on the client company's needs and the available temporary work pool. Temporary employees are carefully selected to match the client's requirements. If you are offered an assignment, you will be told the type of work, longevity, and pay rate. If you accept, you will be required to fill out a weekly time card, verified by the client company, to receive your pay from the temp.

The temp needs to provide a substitute when you are unavailable. You must keep it advised of any emergency preventing your fulfilling your obligations to the customer.

Professional Temporaries

Professional temporaries now include doctors and lawyers. In Atlanta, Locum Tenens (see Resources), founded in 1983, has more than 2,000 doctors on call. Lawsmiths, a San Francisco legal temporary service and one of the nation's leading legal temps, has more than 300 lawyers.

Locum Tenens was one of the first services of this type. Now there are several others. The two major competitors are Comp Help of Salt Lake City and Krone of Chapel Hill, North Carolina.

Locum Tenens doctors go to clients all over the country, with the client providing transportation and housing for the doctor at its site. Locum Tenens pays the doctor's malpractice insurance, a most attractive benefit, and any out-of-state licensing or other required fees.

Edna Maleson, public relations consultant of Locum Tenens, provided several examples of the advantages doctors find working part-time with Locum Tenens.

Dr. Gerson S. Paul retired from a Philadelphia obstetrical practice. "For years I looked forward to retirement, but I hated it," he said. He now works nine months a year for Locum Tenens and spends three months at his home in the Caribbean.

Dr. R.H. Moorman, a general surgeon, retired from his practice in 1989 and registered with Locum Tenens for temporary assignments. He has filled in for a number of doctors in local communities during their vacations. Dr. Moorman says, "I can't picture a life without being a physician."

Locum Tenens conducts a very thorough check to make certain physicians are qualified to be one of its doctors. It researches the doctor's background, including references, the medical boards where licensed, and the AMA. It welcomes older doctors. Most doctors register with Locum Tenens after they leave residency or after they retire.

Lawsmiths is a pioneer in the temporary lawyer help service field. Since Lawsmiths began in 1985, this type of service has become more common, with several firms opening in San Francisco and others springing up in the major metropolitan centers of the country.

Corporate Staff, in San Francisco, provides practically any type of short-term executive or manager a company may need. It works with a nationwide pool of more than 3,500 very capable retired managers and executives who enjoy short-term challenges. The firm, started in 1984, is one of the first temps in the nation to handle executives and managers. Others can now be found in all major cities.

Steve Pickford is an example of persons providing short-term executive expertise. He worked two months as an interim executive on the corporate staff of a large retirement community. Functioning as the personnel director, he successfully recruited a director of human resources and a director of facilities for the organization.

Accountemps, a subsidiary of Robert Half International, specializes in financial professionals and executives. It provides financial managers, CPAs, tax consultants, cost accountants, and bookkeepers. It has more than 100 offices in the U.S., Canada, Britain, and Israel.

It's a Growth Industry

The National Association of Temporary Services projects this industry will grow 5-10 percent a year until the year 2000.

Office workers account for 63 percent of the temporary workload, but the other temporary help specialties are gaining ground in every conceivable skill and work category.

The Bureau of Labor Statistics estimates 98 percent of all U.S. companies use temporaries. Companies see temporaries as a ready labor pool to take care of the sudden and changing needs of the corporation without enlarging the staff. The high cost of benefits and training makes the use of temporary services very attractive to corporations.

According to the February 15, 1988, *Fortune* magazine article, "Smart New Ways to Use Temps," by David Kirkpatrick, Apple Computer uses temporaries to avoid layoffs. Currently 17 percent of its work force consists of transient workers to provide a buffer protecting Apple's permanent staff. Apple made this policy change following the torturous 1985 layoff of 1,200 people brought about by a personal computer industry slowdown.

According to the Bureau of Labor Statistics, the temporary help industry more than doubled between 1982 and 1988, with the number of employees increasing from 400,000 to 1,000,000. Workers aged fifty-five and over accounted for 9.7 percent of temporary workers in 1989. Retirees represent the fastest growing segment of the temporary help services, according to a study by Temps & Company, a national personnel service corporation.

Welcome, Older Workers

The temporary help industry actively seeks retired workers. Many customers prefer them for the same reasons they hire them directly. They know the job, have an excellent work ethic, are responsible, and have good attendance records.

The myth that older workers miss work because of sickness more than younger workers is not true. A Bureau of National Affairs survey shows older workers lose fewer sick days on the job each year. It found workers aged eighteen to forty-four average 3.3 sick days a year while those aged forty-five and over average 2.6 sick days a year. Retirees give a good day's work and are willing to work the odd shifts and cover during vacations. The temps find them to be skilled, responsible, and cooperative.

Kelly Services recruits those aged fifty-five and over and offers training in computers, research, and office management. Kelly Services began the Encore Program in 1988 for recruiting people aged fifty-five and older to return to the work force as temporary workers.

Thomas Temporaries President Bonnie Nash says, "I speak for the industry at large when I say we do a great deal of recruiting for what we describe as the senior market. We attend senior job fairs, advertise in senior publications, go to community and senior centers, and work with government agencies in the pursuit of older workers. We welcome the retiree with open arms."

Florence Mason, a retired hospital personnel director, found the temporaries neither age-conscious nor concerned about overqualification. She performed office work for Kelly Services. "They were great," she said, "I could have worked for them as long as I wanted."

Perfect for Retirees

Temporary work services (temps) are perfect for the retiree. It's as if they were created specifically to fit the lifestyle of those who want a working retirement career that combines the best of work with the best of leisure.

Retirees are attracted to the temps as a way to get out into the world doing something worthwhile, developing new friendships, and supplementing their retirement income.

The temps offer flexibility. Many retirees may wish to work several days a week, work for several weeks, or work only a month or two, and this is easily arranged. Other advantages include freedom of movement and the common practice of registering with several agencies to improve work availability and flexibility. You decide when, where, and how often you want to work. Some temps also provide training.

Temporary help services present a quick route to employment. They offer a variety of career opportunities working for different companies. Retirees can gain experience and skills through a variety of job assignments and work environments, skills difficult to learn when working for a single company. Working for temps is an excellent path to full employment for the company of your choice.

Benefits vary from agency to agency. All are required to meet state and federal requirements for worker's compensation, unemployment compensation contributions, and Social Security. Some provide only the bare minimum of benefits, while others give a full range including paid vacations and holidays, life and health insurance, profit-sharing, and merit raises and bonuses. However, for many retirees the benefits may be of less concern, especially for those already covered by adequate retirement benefits.

Training varies between services from a great deal to none at all. Commonly, computer training includes data entry and word processing, and cross-training on word-processing software.

A 1989 National Association of Temporary Services survey of 2,508 temporary employees found they gave these reasons for working for the temps: Additional income, 80 percent; flexible work schedule, 77 percent; improve skills, 70 percent. Sixty-seven percent gained new skills and 87 percent of the skills gained were computer skills. Sixty-seven percent were seeking a path to a full-time job, and 54 percent had been offered a permanent job by the company.

In 1990 the percentage distribution of temporary help workers was as follows:

★ 63.5 percent office and clerical positions of all types and skill levels.

★ 15.4 percent light and heavy industrial work such as warehouse, assembly work, demonstrations, and janitorial.

★ 11.2 percent technical and professional such as lawyers, engineers, accountants, programmers, and writers.

★ 9.9 percent medical field including doctors, nurses, orderlies, and lab technicians.

Requirements for Registering

A general temporary service is a great place for the widowed homemaker who has either never worked outside her home or has been absent from the work place for many years. Prior formal job experience is not a requirement. Instead, temporary help is selected on the basis of a series of basic skills tests, and many of the skills learned by managing a home and family are applicable.

Such agencies provide workers for the office including receptionists, clerks, typists, secretaries, and those doing light bookkeeping, data entry, and word processing. They also handle light industrial work:

warehousemen, assemblers, and laborers, and those handling shipping, receiving, and inventory.

Thomas Temporaries President Bonnie Nash said, "Our prospective temporaries are selected on the basis of a basic skills test lasting one to one and one-half hours. We primarily want to see if they're responsible and can do the work, not how they gained their skills."

Tests are tailored to the type of job being sought. For office workers, the tests might be filing, typing, following directions, formatting business letters, and spelling. For light bookkeeping, perhaps the ability to strike a trial balance and skills in simple bookkeeping functions would be tested. Applicants are then interviewed to determine their interests, what type of work they want to do, and when and how often they want to work.

When a customer requests help, the temp selects workers from the pool of registered applicants. "It's our job to know both our clients and temporary workers, to assure a good match," Ms. Nash said. "We couldn't stay in business if we failed to do that."

The technical, professional, and executive temporary services have more stringent requirements. They demand the credentials sought by any hiring authority. Resumes, in-depth interviews, and references are used to prove a work history. They also require a letter explaining the worker's interests and availability. If you are accepted, you are interviewed for a temporary position, and if all goes well, you are selected.

Walt Butler networked through a friend whose company needed a job shop engineer to head a complex development project. Walt got the job through the temporary help service that held the help contract for the position. Walt said, "I made 40 percent more money as a temporary than when working directly for a company." Most temporary projects are three months or less. Walt's was a two-year project.

Accounting Solutions, a San Francisco temp, provides temporary service to the industry but uses a staff of mostly permanent financial wizards. It has attracted a talented group of accountants and other financial professionals through a profit-sharing plan that results in salaries averaging 20 percent higher than those offered persons performing similar full-time work. Its expertise is solving management's financial problems. All employees have over a dozen years of experience, and most have stayed with the firm since coming aboard.

Your local telephone Yellow Pages are the best place to find the temp you want. If you can't find it there, contact the National Association of Temporary Services (NATS) (see Resources).

Part-Time Work

Throughout America, companies are beginning to seek retirees for part-time work. Early retirements have often siphoned off some of the more experienced and knowledgeable company employees so the same employees are hired for special projects and to help an overburdened staff when the workload is heavy. Retirees are also used during vacation periods.

The Bureau of Labor Statistics corroborates that employers are using more part-time older workers. Between 1989 and 1990, the number of part-time workers increased 7 percent, to approximately 19.8 million workers, and older workers made up 18.2 percent of that work force. Women account for two-thirds of all part-time and temporary workers.

The service industries, and especially the fast food industry, are the most open to hiring the older worker. McDonald's actively advertises for, trains, and allows retirees to define their own work hours. Kentucky Fried Chicken has similar programs, and most other fast food restaurants seek retirees for part-time help.

The lodging industry also wants the older workers. Roger A. Sanders, president of the American Hotel and Motel Association, urges retirees to take advantage of the full-time, part-time, and flex-time job opportunities. Workers can often arrange their hours to suit their individual requirements.

Insurance Jobs

The Travelers Insurance Company of Hartford started a job bank of retirees for part-time work in 1981. Its needs for these people increased, so in 1985 Travelers began recruiting retirees from other insurance companies. In 1990, it had 120 of its own and sixty from other companies working part-time. Other insurance companies have since begun their own programs.

Rehearsal Retirement is a program initiated by Polaroid of Cambridge, Massachusetts. Workers may try retirement. If they don't like it, they may return to work. The company also provides subsidized education for retirees who have been with the company for ten years or longer and want to enter teaching careers in elementary and secondary schools. Polaroid pays a year's tuition to either Harvard or Lesley College for those retirees.

Aerospace Corporation of Southern California developed a program called Casual Employment. It allows retired Aerospace employees to work up to 1,000 part-time hours a year without losing pension benefits. About 25 percent of their retirees return to work each year on a part-time basis. Some work the full 1,000 hours and others work only during vacation relief.

IBM's practice of taking back IBM retirees to fulfill critical jobs, part-time, benefits both. IBM covers critical jobs or special projects with skilled ex-employees, and retirees once again have an opportunity to exercise career skills. IBM doesn't need to provide special benefits because the retiree still retains company benefits when retired.

If you are near or below the poverty line, you may be eligible for a part-time federal public service job. The Senior Community Service Employment Program (SCSEP) provides part-time employment for low-income unemployed seniors. To be eligible, you must be age fifty-five or older, have an income of no more than 125 percent of the poverty level, and be unemployed. The federal program is administered by the U.S. Department of Labor through national organizations and state agencies. You can find the SCSEP in your area through your local Agency on Aging in the telephone book white pages.

The minimum-wage, public service jobs average twenty to twenty-five hours a week, and are in education and social services, such things as elderly nutrition programs. The bulk of the participants are women; one-third are minorities, one-half have less than a high school education, and one-fourth are age seventy or older.

Part-time work is popular because it allows you to do worthwhile work and meet with others, and the lower earnings don't impact your Social Security income as much. Many continue to enjoy full benefits and work too.

For those under age sixty-five, Social Security benefits are reduced $1 for every $2 earned over a yearly cap of $6,840 per year. The cap is $9,360 for age sixty-five to sixty-nine. Those seventy and above are exempt from any earnings test. Congress is being pressured to remove the Social Security earning penalties to encourage older workers to return to the labor pool. To keep updated on Social Security regulations, Williamson Publishing has an annual edition of Faustin Jehle's *The Complete & Easy Guide to Social Security & Medicare* for $10.95 (800-234-8791).

Working part-time has its negative side. Workers have less job security, pay rates may be less for comparable work, and frequently fringe benefits are not given or are less than for those working full-time. Unemployment benefits are given to part-timers in only six states.

Shared Work

Employers are experimenting with shared work. In this, two people share the same job by working alternate days or weeks, allowing each an opportunity to follow other pursuits and still fulfill the obligations of a full-time job.

Barbara and Susann, two mature museum training coordinators, alternate with one another; each works two days one week and three days the next. They use tape-recorded messages to maintain contact. It works well for them and satisfies the museum's training requirements.

Chapter Twelve

Consulting and

Other Opportunities

It is the great triumph of genius to make the common appear novel. — Johann W. von Goethe (1749-1832)

A consultant provides technical or professional custom services to a customer for a fee. One of the beauties of doing this work is being free to work as often or little as you wish. Such flexibility has great appeal for the retired.

As with temporary help services, age discrimination is not a problem. Many companies prefer and actively seek out older consultants. This is especially true for retirees who offer consulting services to a prior employer, because they understand the company and its policies and know the work.

Another plus for the consultant is that the industry is free from cyclical economic swings. A strong economy turns on the money spigot because clients have plenty of it to hire outside help. Conversely, a weak economy encourages the hiring of outside help to streamline operations, eliminating the costly step of hiring and training employees.

Consulting comes easiest for those treading an old and familiar path. Having a former employer as a ready customer is a good way to start. It encourages other customers once you have gained an established track record with credibility. Your chief assets, as a consultant, are your skills and knowledge of the profession.

Consulting offers self-employment, working out of your own home, and with little or no investment. It allows you to work part-time at your discretion, using your skills and industry contacts. It's no wonder so many retirees become consultants.

Retiree Dick O'Neill, a Silicon Valley consultant, said it best: "Consulting allows me to keep my finger in when I want to, without the stress of a 'have-to' job."

Lyle Samuelson retired from the FBI in 1977. Thirty-six years as a field agent qualified him for all types of security consulting. Since retirement, Lyle has been a consultant to major corporations concerned about security of proprietary information. "I perform investigations for companies guarding against thefts of their product ideas. I turn down more work than I do. It's great to be able to work only when you want to," he said.

Companies use retirees to meet deadlines, to fulfill skills the company lacks, to cover understaffing, to provide an objective third-person viewpoint from outside the company, and to handle sensitive and politically charged situations that are better handled by an outside source.

Federal agencies represent a $3 billion yearly consulting market.

Skills for the Consultant

If you are seriously considering consulting, make certain your capabilities are compatible with consulting type work. Aside from the technical or professional skills, you also need other very important personal attributes and skills if you hope to succeed.

Not everyone can handle being a consultant. It's a loner type job requiring being a motivated self-starter. You need to be comfortable approaching people and selling yourself and your ideas. The retirees who are most successful are those who pursue old career skills with their former employer, then expand to other companies as they gain momentum and experience.

You must be able to get along well with others, to instill confidence and gain cooperation. You must be an excellent communicator both orally and in writing. A consultant's time is filled with putting forth ideas, making presentations, and writing proposals, procedures, and reports. Part of being a good communicator means being a good listener. Communication is a two-way channel; you must listen effectively in order to communicate effectively.

It takes self-discipline to be a consultant, for you're out there alone, making your own opportunities. You must be able to accept rejection, because some will reject you and your advice. And you need the administrative and business skills to make your practice profitable.

Retirees who turn to consulting find that their new role is quite different from that enjoyed as employees. They no longer have the authority to make decisions or direct people to get the job done.

Stan Butler, a retired machine shop manager for the Stanford Linear Accelerator Center (SLAC), returned as a consultant to advise SLAC on bids in the manufacture of close tolerance components. He enjoyed the job and the money, but found his new role as an advisor instead of that of a "mover and shaker," a bit frustrating.

"I didn't have the clout," he said. "It really ticked me off to see them waste time on the wrong things, and I couldn't do anything about it."

You May Have Options

Most retirees go into consulting using career skills, usually with their old employer as their first customer. Some take an entirely new path, away from their previous career, seeking a new and different clientele. Don't overlook your options. Just because you were an outstanding programmer or a great engineer is no reason why you shouldn't pursue other consulting lines of work. It may be more interesting or gratifying for you to take up consulting using a different skill or interest. Or perhaps you will want to use your previous career expertise with some other skill.

Getting Started

Before you begin consulting, you should make some firm decisions by answering these questions:

Do you want a full- or part-time commitment? Will the clients be coming to your office or will you be going to theirs? Who will be your clients and how will you market to them? What equipment will you need? What licenses and permits? Will you need any insurance or bonding? What will you charge for your services?

Most beginning consultants open offices in their homes and many continue there, and for good reason – it keeps their costs down. Also, the office location generally is not important to the customers since your contact with them is either at their place of business or over the phone.

A home-based consulting service may be impractical for you. Perhaps you don't work well with the distractions of family or friends nearby. Often people regard your office in the home different from the standard business office and clog your working hours with non-business interruptions. Also, many people are better motivated if they must report to an office away from the home. If you need an office elsewhere, you have three possible choices: a convenience office, a shared office, or a private office.

A convenience office is working space within a complex of other offices sharing a common reception area. Each office is separate but shares typing, copying, phone answering, conference rooms, and other office amenities. Some even offer accounting services. Renting a convenience office can be an effective way to gain a remote office with a support staff at a lower cost than for a single office with comparable support services.

Shared office space involves sharing space with another consultant. Choose one who complements your business and is not a competitor. You may benefit, not only through the sharing of expenses but also through the contacts and business referrals each may direct to the other. Of course it's important that you are both compatible professionally and personally.

A private office is the most expensive commitment but offers the greatest control. You aren't required to make compromises with anyone except yourself and your pocketbook. You can save money when starting out by using an answering machine in lieu of an answering service, and having typing, copying, and bookkeeping services handled part-time outside the office.

Licenses and Permits

If your consulting work is regulated by your state standards, you may need a license. Such licenses require proven competency. Accountants, engineers, and health services are among those that require such licensing. Check with your state's department of consumer affairs.

You will probably need a business license, even if you use your own home. These are generally issued by the city or county where you live. They are inexpensive. Contact the city clerk's office in your area to see if you need one.

Unless you use your own name for the business, you may have to file with your county clerk for using a fictitious name. The purpose is to identify you to the public by publication in a general circulation newspaper. The cost is minimal.

You may need a seller's permit to sell products. These permits are required in all states that collect retail sales taxes. As a seller, you are authorized to collect retail sales taxes and forward them to the state. A seller's permit exempts you from paying any sales tax on purchases for resale, and allows you to purchase supplies at wholesale prices. The seller's permit is free; however, you may be required to post a bond based on a year's estimated gross sales. Check with your state's tax board.

Consulting Fees

Consultants charge for their services in several ways; by an hourly rate, per project, and by retainer are the most common. Experts say a fixed price per project is preferred by clients and the most profitable for you.

What you can charge will depend on your expertise, service exclusiveness, personal reputation, record of achievements and credentials, market effectiveness, and, most important, your value to the customer.

To be profitable, your consulting fee must consider four major areas: salary, overhead, profit, and the competition.

■ **Salary.** Set your salary based on what others doing similar work are being paid.

■ **Overhead.** Overhead is the cost of doing business and must include all the direct and indirect costs associated with it. These include rent, utilities, telephone, supplies, outside support services, advertising, promotion, and any other costs of running the business. Your business expenses are either customer-related or general expenses. All customer-related expenses are charged directly to the customer in addition to the consulting fee. The general business costs, such as rent and utilities, are covered by your fees.

■ **Profit.** Your fee should include a profit margin above the combined cost of salary and overhead. Many people ignore either the salary or the profit in calculating their fees, mistakenly believing them to be the same thing. Not true. Both must be considered in setting fees.

■ **Competition.** You're not the only consulting firm of your type. Check the competition. Knowing and understanding your competitors and how they figure their costs and fees is essential. Find out how they charge for their services. Learn what kind of overhead they have in relation to yours.

Networking with your peers is the best way to find out what works and the best way to keep tabs on what's going on in the industry. Join a consulting professional association. You'll find them listed in the *Gale's Encyclopedia of Associations* at your library.

Discovering the fee range for your type of consulting service allows you to decide intelligently where to set your fees, based on your salary, your overhead, and your profit expectations in relation to the competition.

The value of any service, in the final analysis, is determined by the amount buyers are willing to pay. It's what the customer perceives as the best price for the quality received. Clients are always willing to sacrifice price for what they consider the best. It's your job to convince them you're the best at any price.

Marketing Your Services

Understanding your customers and how to appeal to their needs and emotions is critical to sales success.

To sell successfully, ask your clients these questions and learn from their answers: What's important to you? What would you like to see? What is your biggest problem? Then examine your product or service for advantages and benefits for the user. Sell what it will do for them, not for what it is. Tire salesmen sell safety, not tires. Insurance salesman sell peace of mind, not insurance. You, too, must sell the benefits, not the features.

Marketing Strategies

The three main marketing strategies are networking, publicity, and advertising.

■ **Networking.** Networking is perhaps the most productive of the three. This is especially true if you are a consultant picking up where you left off with your old employer. Through your contacts with career colleagues and friends, you begin by building a reputation and business with your prior employer and follow through by expanding to other parts of the industry.

Your network should include membership in at least two associations, a trade or professional association and a consultant's association. Getting involved in associations is an invaluable aid for getting exposure and rubbing shoulders with the ones who are in a position to help you the most. Check the *Gale's Encyclopedia of Associations* at your local library for help. Joining community and business groups such as the Lions Club, Chamber of Commerce, and Women in Business is also important.

■ **Publicity.** Making speeches and giving seminars expand your network and bring in prospects by giving you an image as an expert.

Being an expert or having an unusual consulting service makes you newsworthy. The free publicity of newspaper, radio, or television interviews is the best kind of advertisement, the kind that lends you great credibility and can be referenced in your sales brochure.

Writing articles for magazines and newspapers is an excellent way to gain free publicity and advance your image as an expert. This is especially productive when you are writing for professional and trade magazines devoted to areas of your clients' interest. Publishing your own newsletter is another excellent way to reach and expand a customer base.

■ **Advertising.** Successful advertising means attracting your customers at the least cost.

At the beginning your advertising may be strictly word-of-mouth, gaining new business through satisfied customer referrals. Business cards are an excellent, inexpensive means of spreading the word to everyone you meet.

A telephone Yellow Page listing is very effective for most businesses. This is included in your business phone charges. Ad enhancements are extra. They include bold face type and additional words. Of course, you can go for the large column or display ads too, but they may not be necessary, and once the ad is in the book you're obligated for the year.

Thirty percent of all advertising in the United States is done through the newspapers. Newspaper advertising is appealing because of the low cost per the number of people reached. And the papers include a relatively inexpensive classified section. The classified can be beneficial for many. I did well with my career consulting service in the classifieds. It may or may not be valid for your type of service. A display ad in other sections of the paper may prove more appropriate. For example, if you are a food caterer, try the food section, and if you are a computer professional, use the business section.

Trade and professional magazines are often an excellent advertising choice because of their select audience. Your ad reaches exactly those who are most likely to be interested in your consulting service. These periodicals are very good for marketing newsletters, books, and audio/video tapes.

Radio and television are also possible sources for advertising and have been successful for some. However, we're talking big bucks here. Not a recommended choice to start with.

Many are successful with direct mail advertisements selling books, newsletters, and self-help audio-video tapes to a select list of prospective customers. However, direct mail is expensive and the responses are low. They normally range from less than 1 percent to 3 percent of the mailing. Experts agree that the proper list is crucial to direct mail success. The best mailing of all is your own list of proven past users of your service. Be aware that direct mail requires considerable expertise to be successful and that even the experts often suffer failures.

Seminars and Newsletters

Conducting seminars and publishing newsletters are two important means of furthering a consulting business while increasing your income.

The U.S. seminar industry is a six-billion-dollar a year business. There are seminars on almost any subject. People are attracted to seminars for a variety of reasons: to get specialized information quickly, to talk with the distinguished presenters, for a change of scenery in an attractive setting, or to get the handout material and manuals unavailable elsewhere. Many attend because they believe they could not gain the same information through their own efforts.

Seminars attract two different groups. One is made up of people whose organizations pay to have their employees/members upgraded. The other consists of people who pay their own way.

The fee structures for each are quite different. The seminars aimed at organizations may cost as much as $200-$500 a day, whereas seminars for individuals generally run as low as $25 to $50 per day. The subjects, too, also differ. Those directed toward organizations for improving their employees offer instruction in job-related skills such as dealing with customers. Seminars dealing with individuals involve subjects that are important to the individuals personally, such as how to make more money and self-improvement.

Conducting successful seminars — and this of course can be a business on its own — can benefit you in three ways: the seminar adds income, those attending become excellent prospects for your consulting services, and seminars enhance your professional image in the industry.

Seminars are excellent opportunities for selling audio and video cassette tapes of the seminar content. Many sell cassette tapes for prices approaching those paid by the persons who attended. Books on the seminar subject also sell well. This is especially profitable if you're the author. You gain financially and receive recognition as an expert.

Successful seminars are those that leave those attending with something they consider new, valuable, and useful. It must be a benefit that can be acquired within the short time span of the seminar presentation, and it must have sufficient worth to justify the expense and inconvenience of attending. It also must be something that could not be easily acquired in some other way or from some other more convenient source. Find a niche and fill it.

Consulting Products

The hours you can spend providing a consulting service limit the amount of money you can make. No such limits are encountered when selling a product. It's open-ended. Limitless.

Newsletters, how-to books, and video and audio tapes are products that can be sold to an open-ended audience. Seminars and lecture tours are a good forum for launching and promoting such products.

Newsletters have two to ten pages and provide valuable and often unique information to a targeted audience. They are published weekly, monthly, and quarterly. Most common are monthly publications.

Newsletters are popular with consulting customers because they provide specialized information and help, often not available elsewhere. The more specialized and less general the information, the more attractive the newsletter is for those who need that information.

Some consultants publish a free newsletter for clients and prospective clients. Most, however, use the newsletter as another source of income; sometimes it becomes more lucrative than the consulting service.

Newsletter prices are determined by the uniqueness of the newsletter and its value to the user. If you publish the only information on an important subject needed by a given group, you can command a high price for newsletter subscriptions. The greater the value to the reader, the higher the price you can charge.

A newsletter does not need to be professionally printed to be successful. Many expensive and highly successful newsletters were typewritten and copied, rather than professionally printed. The newsletter subscriber buys information and advice, not appearance. If you own a personal computer, a printer, and word-processing software or, better yet, desk top publishing software, you can easily produce an attractive newsletter.

Selling Other Products

■ **Books.** Writing a book, although time-consuming, can be both financially rewarding and a boost to the prestige and professional credibility of the author. You are seen as an expert, increasing your visibility and desirability in the marketplace.

The two paths to publication are self-publishing or selling your book proposal idea to a non-fiction book publishing firm.

Self-publishing requires you to pay the entire expense of publishing and marketing the book. However, you retain control of the process and receive all of the profits or suffer all of the loss. A market plan is essential.

Getting a publisher to publish your book requires selling the idea, then negotiating the manner in which the book will be written and produced. The author does not invest any money and receives a negotiated royalty on each book sold or sells the book outright to the publishing firm. Either way it is an arduous, time-consuming process.

■ **Audio-video Cassettes.** Not everyone will attend your seminar or lecture, but many would purchase a recording of the material. Many of the recordings are simply edited versions of a presentation. Cassettes are generally sold in sets made up into a booklike package complete with a flyer explaining the material.

Audio cassettes are easier and less expensive to develop. You can listen to audio recordings used anywhere – while traveling in a car, while using a Walkman, or in the comfort of your home.

Other Help Available

Howard L. Shenson, a certified management consultant (CMC), is one of the leaders of the consulting industry. He specializes in marketing professional practices and information services on seminars, newsletters, and consulting. Those serious about consulting may wish to contact him about his educational packages.

A number of books on consulting are available including *Advice, a High Profit Business, Marketing with Seminars and Newsletters,* and *The Consultant's Guide to Winning Clients,* all by Herman Holtz; *Cashing in on the Consulting Boom* by Kishel and Gunter, and *How to Create and Market a Successful Seminar or Workshop* by Howard Shenson.

Check the *Gale's Encyclopedia of Associations* for consulting associations of your choice.

In summary, if you have the temperament for it, consulting can be a most satisfying retirement career, one that possesses the golden ingredients of challenging work spiced with recreation and leisure. Consulting allows you to decide when and how often you want to be involved. Perhaps it is right for you.

Chapter Thirteen

Starting a
Home Business

To be a success in business, be daring, be first, be different.
— Marchant

Have you ever wanted to be your own boss, to go into business for yourself? Most people have. Now, when you're retired, is a good time to try it. The least painful method is to start a home-based business, one that allows you to dip a toe in to test the water before jumping in all the way.

If you want a business, a home-based business may be your perfect retirement career. It can be a flexible way to stay involved and interested, and will provide plenty of challenges. It can be a part-time involvement conveniently blended around other retirement activities or it can be a full-fledged, fiercely competitive, all-absorbing business. It's your choice.

There are more than 13 million businesses in the United States. The Small Business Administration says 97 percent of them are small businesses, 79 percent of which are home-based. A 1986 AT&T survey found 41 percent of the home businesses made over $30,000 per year.

The most successful businesses fulfill special needs. Try to find some unique angle that will give you an advantage. Discover something different or a new twist to an old product or service. Think like a customer. Why would you, as a customer, want to buy your product or use your service instead of going to all those already in business? If you can't answer that maybe you should try something else.

My home-based career consulting business didn't start taking off until I started interviewing resume clients by phone instead of in person. It was a brand new wrinkle, providing a desirable service, and it didn't require impressive surroundings.

Home businesses are as varied as the imagination can conjure up. To determine what type of business would suit you best, examine your hobbies, your job-related activities, and those areas of need for a product or service you would like to provide. Pick something you like to do and can do well. Even the less talented of us do those things well that we enjoy, and why would you want to saddle yourself with a hateful task anyway? A home business should be fun, especially now that you're retired and have the freedom to choose from your options.

No matter how talented you are, unless there is a market for what you have to offer, you won't succeed. Check to see if similar businesses exist. If not, perhaps there is a good reason why not. There may not be a market for it. Of course there is always the possibility you're the first to recognize a need and are in on the ground floor, but don't bet on it without first testing to make certain.

Retirees from all walks of life operate home businesses. A retired Florida car salesman repairs golf clubs as a part-time home business. It gives him a small income, something to do he enjoys, and time for the fun and freedom to play his favorite game. Golf.

A California homemaker turned her green thumb ability into a home business for designing and maintaining company flower beds in an industrial park. She uses students for part-time help.

A bank manager, displaced by a merger, retired to the Mendocino coast to make and sell custom jewelry in his home workshop overlooking the sea.

A Wisconsin real estate developer retiree, an avid fisherman, designs and sells fishing lures from his home to markets throughout the United States and Canada.

A sixty-year-old New Mexico woman started a house-sitting service for vacationers. She operates a contract referral system from her home, using retirees for sitters. They live in to look after things, feed the pets, water the plants, and do light maintenance.

An eighty-six-year-old California woman tole paints wedding and graduation plaques. She mounts wedding and graduation announcements on carved wooden plaques and then decorates them with colorful tole paintings. Her reputation has exceeded her ability to satisfy the demand.

A former high school wood shop instructor builds exquisite inlaid coffee tables and end tables of colorful and expensive woods for sale in his home workshop.

A seventy-two-year-old retired New Jersey accountant operates a home-based tax service for local small businesses. He uses a PC computer.

Advantages of a Home-Based Business

Self-starters who enjoy the work they do, working independently in an unstructured environment, are the most comfortable home business entrepreneurs.

A home business offers many advantages, such as being your own boss with the flexibility to make your own decisions.

You'll also avoid the costs of owning, leasing, or renting an expensive separate place of business and gain the lower overhead costs of sharing utilities in the home. Converting part of your household expenses to business expenses allows you to try a new business without a substantial financial risk.

Working at home eliminates that daily commute and allows you to dress casually, thus cutting your spending on clothing.

Home-based businesses can be a wonderful opportunity for a husband and wife to work in a business together. For example, the husband may have the professional expertise for satisfying the customer's needs but lack the administrative attributes necessary to run a profitable business. If the wife has those skills, it makes a great combination for a satisfying partnership.

Hayden Waymore, a retired Air Force sergeant, started a home-based mobile diesel truck repair service. Hayden is an excellent mechanic, but he isn't comfortable with the administrative side of the business, especially when it involves collecting delinquent accounts. His wife, a retired school teacher, has a good head for business and no problems at all collecting past due accounts. This is an unbeatable combination for a successful husband and wife enterprise.

A husband and wife team can have its pitfalls. Being constantly thrown together, both at work and play without relief from one another, can strain a relationship to the breaking point. Such business partnerships work best when, like Hayden and his wife, each performs specific functions separate from one another at least part of the time.

The Downside of It

A home-based business isn't for everyone. It can be lonely by yourself. Many people miss working in a group environment. They need the stimulus of regular hours at a specified location away from home. If you were one of those people who enjoyed the action at the office, the morning coffee klatches, and the lunches with fellow workers as much as the work itself, a home-based business may not work for you.

Some things can prove to be problems. Does your home have adequate space for your needs? Do the zoning laws permit your type of business activities in your home? Will your neighbors pose a problem? How will your family or spouse react to a business in the home? Will the constant contact of husband and wife be a problem? How will your customers react to coming to your home to do business?

People who work for themselves usually work longer hours than they did when working for an employer. It's hard to get away from your work when you live with it. It means learning to manage your time effectively to be successful. Your income may be sporadic, flush one moment and broke or bent the next, and no one is looking after your fringe benefits except you. Also, if something goes wrong, there's no one to turn to for help.

Family and friends may take a home-based business lightly, thinking nothing of interrupting you for any and every mundane reason, something they wouldn't do if your office were uptown.

My home-based business of writing resumes suffered image problems until I initiated telephone interviews. It proved to be more convenient and very popular, countering the negative image people had of being interviewed in my home.

Assess how supportive your spouse and family will be toward a home-based business. Household members may not wish to accept a pinch in finances, your long working hours, and having to share in the work when they would rather be doing something else.

A spouse can be a problem for the home-based operator because of the continual association all day, every day. Togetherness may be a blessing for some and a curse for others, giving one a feeling of never having a private life. Smart home business owners establish off-limit areas for business purposes and maintain a work schedule for the business day. Such actions separate business operations from the household.

Diversify

Explore whatever business idea you decide upon for the many and varied ways it can be exploited as a business. You may be pleasantly surprised at the different avenues for profit that exist.

I wanted to start a retirement career as a writer. Writing for money is not the easiest of careers for achieving financial success. The typical free-lance writer averages somewhere between $5,000 and $7,000 a year. Not a very awe-inspiring sum.

Writers can improve their financial rewards tremendously if they are willing to use their writing talents in several ways. The *Writer's Market* suggests the fees to charge for 223 ways writers can make money from their craft.

To a greater or lesser degree, what is true for writers is also true for other disciplines. Don't fail to explore all your possibilities.

Advice on Home Businesses

The business scene is a demanding, unforgiving place; therefore, being very good at what you do is important to success. You have to be good to be a viable competitor, and enjoying what you do to the point of doing it even if you didn't have to, will help keep you going when times are rough.

Working for yourself demands being organized and a self-starter. It takes self-discipline to do what has to be done, especially when the sky is that certain shade of blue and the fragrance of spring beckons. Of course you can succumb to those temptations and make up for them at a later time. That's one of the benefits of working for yourself. But those who are most successful set schedules and keep to them, the same as one would if working for an employer.

I find it works best if I set concrete deadlines for my writing tasks. I allocate so many days to complete a chapter's rough draft and so many days to do the final rewrite. This allows me to be flexible in deciding when I will sit at the word processor and hammer out the work. I try to do the creative part in the morning when I'm at my best. After 2 P.M., I'm not very productive.

Keep your home office or work area isolated from the rest of the house. Even if it's only a small corner of a room, keep it screened off and separate. This is necessary if you want to claim a portion of your home as a business expense for federal income tax purposes. This also gives you a place to schedule and carry out uninterrupted business, a place for privacy.

If possible, set aside a room for your home office. This provides the security of a door and allows the room to take on a more business-like atmosphere. This is doubly important if you receive customers in your home. A separate room removes any possible question the IRS may have concerning exclusive use.

When you think of your business in your home, think of it as your office, not your home, and treat it as such. This will make it easier to keep the distinction straight in your mind so that it will seem more like going to work away from home.

Plan and schedule your work. Most successful home business operators adhere to a daily work schedule. Schedules can be used to minimize household interruptions, making your office off limits during scheduled times. The schedule can be one that fits your own work ethic. Perhaps you work best in the early morning, or maybe you're a late riser and work best later. I have a friend who works from 4:30 until 9:30 each morning, and another who does all his work after 6 P.M. Those are both extremes but it works for them. Of course, if your business is in constant contact with the public, your hours must also accommodate your customers.

Take Time Out

Don't get so wound up in your work that you fail to take time out for other things. Working for yourself can smother you with all work and no play if you let it. Make it a scheduled habit to get out of the house for a change of scenery and exercise at least once a day. My wife and I start our day with a vigorous walk around a local park lake. It's a grand way to get the juices flowing and the cheeks glowing. It's become a daily event that we would hate to give up.

Acquire a business telephone line separate from the house phone.

This has several advantages: A dedicated business phone isolates your office from the home, creating a more businesslike arrangement by eliminating household conversations intermingled with business. A separate phone line allows you to maintain regular daytime office hours by not answering the phone after hours. Also, it provides a Yellow Pages advertisement listing and simplifies phone charges for tax purposes.

Set up a separate bank account for your business. Of course, if your business name is other than your own name, you have to have a business account or you can't cash checks. In either case, you need a business account for record-keeping and for credibility when dealing with customers and other businesses.

Use an answering machine to monitor your calls during off hours or when you're not available during business hours. This is also a great way to screen calls if you're a writer like me and don't want to be interrupted during the writing part of your day.

Have a clear picture of how far you want to go with your home business. Continued growth can push it out of your house and into the corporate world complete with a staff of employees and all of the associated complexities of expansion. If that's what you want, fine. If not, be prepared to cut back or sell out before you reach critical mass.

Marketing

A good product or service will not sell itself. Selling is up to you. Find out how others in your type of business reach their customers, then do the same. Do market research, which is simply finding out what is wanted by whom and where. Check the telephone Yellow Pages. In most cases you'll find a number of similar businesses. Call them and find out all you can about their products or services, what they offer, how much they charge, who their customers are, and how they attract them.

Business cards are an inexpensive method of letting people know about your business, especially when networking. Distribute them to everyone who may be interested. Let them know what you have to offer. Specialized newspaper or magazine advertising is effective when your product or service is of interest to a specialized group.

An ad in the telephone Yellow Pages is an effective way to let those who need your type of business know about you. A listing comes with your business phone; there's a charge for bold type and extra information.

Being smart about your business name can be an advantage. For example, I named my writing service simply "Resume Service." At first glance, it's not a very imaginative name, but it had one big advantage. The company name stood out as the only recognizable resume service in the white pages. Many people look for help in the white pages first, a fact that brought me a lot of business with a simple business phone listing.

Another ploy is the game of trying to be first in the listings. You may have noticed many businesses are named to assure being alphabetically listed near the front, to get your attention and then your business.

Mail order works well for those who have the right mailing list and know the ropes. It requires expertise to be successful and can be very expensive for the uninitiated.

Local newspaper advertising and the classified ads are relatively inexpensive for the number of people reached, and can be very effective if your business is applicable to that style of advertising. Not everyone reads the classified section, but those who do, read it thoroughly. Often the weekend classified section is read more heavily than during the daily section.

You must be able to sell yourself and your business to others. You need to know how you stack up in relation to your competition and how to get your share of the market. Having a unique angle can often give you that little special edge over the rest of the field.

In addition to my career consulting service and writing business resumes, I handled government resumes. A government resume, unlike a standard one-page business resume, is an involved document, frequently requiring fifteen to twenty pages of specialized written narrative. The government's system is laborious and difficult for even the most diligent applicant. My government service gave me an insight into what reviewers were looking for in applicants. I initially researched the competition that advertised in the local military newspaper. My lower overhead allowed me to set lower prices, but it wasn't long before my reputation grew to the point where my prices exceeded those of the competition, and I still had more business than I could handle.

Legal Considerations

Before starting a home business, check with your local city government to be certain your business will be allowed by the zoning laws.

Licensing requirements for businesses vary greatly, depending upon where you live, so check with your city, county, state, and federal agencies.

A city business license is generally required. Get it at the city clerk's office. It should not be expensive.

If you intend to sell a product in a state where sales taxes are collected, you will need a seller's permit. This requires you to collect and forward sales taxes on products you sell. It also allows you to purchase supplies used in products for sale at wholesale prices. Check with your state's tax board to see if you need a seller's permit.

Unless you use your own name for your business, you must register your business name, usually with the county clerk's office. There may be other federal or state licenses required for your unique type of business. Check thoroughly.

Find out from your insurance agent if your homeowner's insurance coverage is sufficient. If not, you may need additional protection.

SBA Development Program

The federal government's Small Business Administration (SBA) has a product development program you should know about. The Small Business Innovation Research (SBIR) program manages money grants provided by eleven federal agencies to small businesses for research and development. To qualify, you must have a product to develop that will be applicable to one of the 1,500 areas of interest controlled by the eleven funding agencies.

Two steps are necessary to receive funding for development. You first must apply for a Phase I award, which is a feasibility study to be completed within six months. Up to $50,000 may be awarded for the study.

If the study results are acceptable to the screening agency, you then may apply for the Phase II funding to do the actual development work. Up to $500,000 may be awarded for a two-year development project. Being accepted to do a Phase I study does not guarantee Phase II funding. Generally, fewer than one-third of the Phase I studies result in a Phase II award.

Don't be intimidated by the thought that everything must be high tech. Some items that qualify are not complicated development projects. For example, the U.S. Department of Education is looking for the development or adaptation of devices or techniques to aid disabled persons in a number of disability areas, such as language, sight, hearing, and ambulatory and mental retardation.

For a complete list of development topics, call your local SBA office for information or write to SBIR Pre-Solicitation Announcements (see Resources).

Hire Professionals

In starting a small business, don't try to do it all yourself. You can't be an expert in all areas, and it's costly to attempt to do those things you are not qualified to do. The cardinal rule of business is do what you're good at and hire experts for what you're not.

Consult professionals when you need help. A good tax accountant can save you money above the cost. You should use one at least in the beginning to teach you the best way to set up your books to satisfy the Internal Revenue Service (IRS). In addition to the direct costs of doing business, the IRS allows you to deduct that part of your home exclusively and regularly used for a business. This includes a percentage of your home depreciation, mortgage interest, real estate taxes, insurance, and utilities. A good tax specialist can save you money and keep you out of trouble with the IRS.

Using a bookkeeper or accountant is a sound practice in the beginning, especially to get you pointed in the right direction. Once your books are set up, perhaps you can go it alone except at tax time.

If you need to draw up contracts for dealing with clients, run them by a lawyer. Specialized needs require specialized pros.

Don't overlook hiring part-time help to relieve you of the mundane tasks that would keep you from concentrating on your important work. A youngster in the neighborhood or perhaps another adult seeking some extra cash can be a great help.

Thoughts on Equipment

Equipping a home office will vary according to the space available and your specific needs, however a few ideas may help stimulate your thoughts on equipping your office.

If you have an office set up in a corner of a room normally used for other living purposes, use screens, room dividers, and bookshelf dividers for some measure of privacy.

A desktop personal computer is a good office companion. It's invaluable for graphics, computer-aided drafting (CAD), accounting, bookkeeping, and for maintaining electronic files and data bases for inventories, products, and customers. It's a must for those who need to do heavy writing chores. Modern word processing and desktop publishing software put the mark of excellence on published works. If space is at a premium, consider a laptop computer, which has the added advantage of portability for use at home or away.

Hanging wall shelves and bulletin boards are handy space savers for your office. Any number of utility desk and file cabinet combinations are available from office supply and major mail order houses and are clever space-savers. For a start, a couple of two-drawer file cabinets with a sheet of plywood between them provide both a desk and filing space.

An answering machine is one of your best investments for keeping tabs on customers when you're unavailable. Purchase one that has a message counter, is voice-activated to store the entire message, and doesn't waste tape or message count by storing "no talk messages."

Machines are also available that contain a phone, a speaker phone, an answering machine, and a computerized address/phone directory, all in one unit.

Tape recorders are valuable little home business tools. I use two of them. I have a standard recorder in my office that can be used with a Radio Shack telephone recording control pickup device for recording interviews over the phone. I also use a small pocket micro cassette recorder for a notebook wherever I go to record those flashes of inspiration that we all get. I used to carry a notebook and pen, but I prefer the micro recorder because I can use it when I'm driving.

Small, inexpensive electronic calculators take up little space and are now available with a miniature printed output for those who need an audit trail.

Most major photocopy manufacturers offer small desk top copiers for under $2,000. At the beginning, though, I recommend using local copy services until your business is large enough to justify your own machine.

Retirement's freedoms and options free you, perhaps for the first time, to be your own boss, to be an entrepreneur, to satisfy a lifelong dream. Now is the time to make that dream a reality.

In your quest for more knowledge, I recommend reading the home-based business industry's recognized reference work, *Working From Home* by Paul and Sarah Edwards. Other recommended reading: *Starting & Operating a Home-Based Business* by David R. Eyler and *The Home-Based Entrepreneur* by Pinson and Jinnett (Out of Your Mind . . . and Into the Marketplace, Tustin, CA).

Chapter Fourteen

Volundering:

Public Service

That Satisfies

There is no higher religion than human service. To work for the common good is the greatest creed. – Albert Schweitzer (1875-1965)

"And so, my fellow Americans, ask not what your country can do for you; ask what you can do for your country." These memorable and stirring words by President John Fitzgerald Kennedy have an important message for you who possess the skills, the creativity, and the time to make a difference.

To volunteer is a basic human trait. America's history is one of volunteering. Neighbors help neighbors by coming to one another's aid in times of crisis; community barn raisings, sharing food and shelter in times of tornado and flood, and helping to harvest the crops are typical early American examples. Today, volunteering is an integral part of both the public and private sectors of our communities. It's been said that at some time during the year, 137 million Americans volunteer in some capacity.

Volunteers are a cost-effective, practical addition to a paid staff, allowing organizations to better serve more people at less cost. Volunteers are not free, however, because they often require training, administration, and support services to be effective. Successful volunteer programs provide services valued many times over the actual investment.

Volunteering is helping yourself by helping others. Today's volunteer has as much to gain from volunteering as those being helped. This is especially true for the retired. It gives you the opportunity to reactivate career skills for the community good. Being needed and making a difference gives meaning to your life. Retirees make some of the best volunteers because of their work ethic and sense of responsibility. They can be counted on and thus are sought after.

Why People Volunteer

There are many reasons to volunteer. Volunteering is both a giving and a receiving; a mixture of the selflessness of helping others and the selfishness of helping yourself. It's a good substitute for working without the encumbrances of making a living.

Many retirees volunteer to fill a void – to have something to do. It gets them out of the house and into the mainstream to meet and socialize with others – a reason to get up and do.

It can also give them a chance to be with and work with younger people, to keep active and young of mind. Fulfilling a needed public service satisfies psychological needs and puts value back into lives.

Marlene Samson volunteered as an aquarium docent because she was lonely and needed something to keep her busy. Her husband died of a heart attack shortly after they relocated to a new area following his retirement. Far removed from her friends and family support system, she felt alone and lost.

"Volunteering was my salvation," she said. "If it hadn't been for my volunteer work, I don't know what would have become of me."

Volunteering gives you the chance to once again practice your career skills or your profession, minus the stress of making a living. Whatever your skills or career background may be, you will find volunteer opportunities to match them.

Can Save Lives

Many volunteers are life savers when catastrophe strikes. Dwayne Eskridge retired in 1977 and became an involved amateur radio volunteer, fulfilling the post of assistant director of the Pacific Division of the American Radio Relay League, a nationwide organization of amateur radio operators. He has jurisdiction over central and northern California and the states of Nevada and Washington.

Mr. Eskridge managed 400-plus volunteer amateur radio operators for fourteen days after the October 17, 1989, earthquake devastated the San Francisco Bay area communities. His group provided all the communications for the Santa Cruz and Watsonville areas immediately following the quake and until adequate phone service was restored. Their outstanding efforts saved lives and provided comfort for the quake victims.

Others volunteer with the altruistic motives to help those less fortunate than themselves. Once retired you may feel, as many before you, that now is the time to give something back to the community by lending a helping hand to the handicapped, the homeless, the sick, the elderly, and the needy. There is no greater service than that performed for the less fortunate, and there's no greater reward than the knowledge that you made a difference in someone's life.

Dorothy Victorino, a retired RN, translates books into Braille for the blind. It's a tedious and exacting volunteer job but she finds satisfaction in the pleasure it brings to those who "see" through touch.

Octogenarian Al Fuchin, a once-a-week Volunteer Peer Counselor, gained his volunteer counseling skills through four months of training from professionals. He learned to counsel seniors about the problems of depression, sickness, and the death of a spouse.

Al also volunteers in other areas: Project Cleanup, making surplus farm foods available to agencies supplying the needy; the Brown Bag Program, providing a weekly bag of groceries for people below the poverty level; and the Family Visitors Program, visiting elderly shut-ins. Al is making a difference, and is determined to spend the rest of his life helping those in need.

He told me about his regular visits sharing interests with a housebound elderly man whose friends had long since passed on. Eventually the man was hospitalized with terminal cancer with no one except Al to visit him.

"The week before he died, we talked quietly about the past, about nostalgic things," Al said. "When I got up to leave, he grasped my arm, squeezing tightly with both hands." Al's voice broke. "I'll never forget that moment."

Learn New Skills

You may have a desire to broaden your horizons by gaining new experiences and learning new things. Volunteering can offer opportunities to learn new skills, to travel new paths. Many organizations provide training for their volunteers, allowing you to start anew. Volunteering allows you to work in new career areas without financial risk.

Mary Craft launched a new career because of her volunteer association with the Monterey Bay Aquarium in California. The aquarium's sea otter rehabilitation program inspired her to watercolor illustrate and self-publish a children's book about orphaned otters. She now is well on her way to selling her writing and watercolor paintings through self-publishing and local gift shops.

Many retired people fail to volunteer because they believe volunteers are not considered to be professionals in the corporate world of work. I don't believe that to be true anymore, and perhaps it was never totally true. It really depends upon the organization and how it views and utilizes its volunteer staff.

The Monterey Bay Aquarium, one of the world's most successful aquariums, owes a large measure of its outstanding success to a huge volunteer staff, a staff exceeding paid employees by three to one. The volunteers ARE the aquarium. Without them it would be just another fish bowl. The volunteer docents are the aquarium's good-will ambassadors. They are the ones who visitors see and interact with daily.

To maintain excellence, the aquarium has a sixteen-week volunteer training program and provides continuous enhancement training to assure a competent volunteer staff. Each volunteer docent's public performance is periodically evaluated by a qualified training coordinator, to counsel those who need improvement and to determine future training program changes.

The aquarium reveres and cherishes its volunteers and treats them as respected professionals.

The Negative Side

Volunteering is not without its downside. Volunteers are sometimes taken for granted and treated as if they were receiving a salary. Some organizations fail to give them enough recognition for their services.

Mary, a northern California parishioner, hates being taken for granted, "I love volunteering for the church," she said, "but nobody ever says anything about what a good job I'm doing. I'm really not getting paid for it, you know."

Some non-profit organizations neglect to reimburse volunteers for their out-of-pocket expenses. Such expenses can be quite formidable. Sara and George, who were members of the board of directors of their church, were frequently requested to meet and entertain visiting church dignitaries, a task they thoroughly enjoyed. "We loved being board members and enjoyed the volunteer work." Sara said. "We would have continued if the church had at least helped with some of the expenses." Thoughtlessness cost the church two of its most valuable volunteer assets. Sara and George have since joined another church, one that appreciates its volunteers.

Inadequate training is sometimes a problem. Volunteers may be asked to perform functions they have not been trained to do. Tasks and duties vary from one organization to another, requiring training. Also, new volunteers need a period of "hand holding" by an experienced person until they are competent in their duties. And emergency situations need to be thoroughly covered so all will know what actions to take during the unexpected.

Frequently, volunteers are called upon to help out in a variety of capacities on an occasional rotating basis. Such actions demand that adequate posted instructions be available to assist them.

Mary Lou, a member and volunteer for an artist association, was asked to open and manage the association facilities during the regular manager's illness. "I had several requests for information I couldn't answer," Mary Lou said. "The information should have been available in written instructions for whoever works the post."

Sometimes organizations fail to take their volunteers seriously, neglecting to take full advantage of their capabilities. And professionals have been known to look down on the volunteer as "just a volunteer." What is even worse, some volunteers view themselves the same way.

Volunteer Protocol

Organizations need volunteers who take their duties seriously, who get the job done, and who see to it that a substitute will carry on when they are unavailable for duty.

If you fail to take your volunteer position seriously, it has little meaning for you and little value for those you serve. It is necessary to view your status with the same importance as a paid position. People rely on you, and therefore you, as a volunteer, should be considerate of time schedules. Know what your job is, and just as important know what your job is not. It's important not to exceed your authority. Good volunteers are well qualified and know their jobs. They also show respect for people of all types and ethnic backgrounds. Leave your prejudices at home when you volunteer because non-profit organizations cater to all types of people, and you will be expected to treat them with respect.

How and Where to Volunteer

A 1985 Gallup survey found only 38 percent of those over the age of sixty-five volunteer, whereas 54 percent of those between the ages of thirty-five and forty-nine do. Why don't more retired people do this? They are the healthiest, best educated, and longest living older population in history. Of course some are unable to volunteer, but many would do so if someone asked them. An American Association of Retired People (AARP) survey found a full 20 percent of those who didn't volunteer were interested in doing so if given the opportunity.

People volunteer in all kinds of areas. Here is how the 1985 Gallup survey found the percentage distribution:

Volunteer Area	Percent
Religious organizations	19.7
Informal – Alone	16.2
Education	11.1
General fund-raisers	9.4
Recreation	8.6
Health	7.7
Civic, social and fraternal organizations.	6.8
Social services and welfare	6.0
Arts and crafts	3.4
Work-related organizations	3.4
Community action	3.4
Political organizations	3.4
Justice	0.9
	100.0

How do retired people find places to volunteer their special skills or desires? If you are age sixty or older and retired or semiretired, your best bet may be the local Retired Senior Volunteer Program (RSVP).

There are over a half million retirees nationwide volunteering their services through over 51,000 local organizations churning out 64 million hours of service every year.

A visit to your local RSVP office will point you toward a type of volunteer activity that may interest you, such as tutoring, coaching, arts and crafts, entertaining, helping the sick and the needy, and docents in museums, zoos, and aquariums. You name it and RSVP will find a volunteer position to fit your needs, often in your own neighborhood. Check your phone book white pages or contact RSVP (see Resources).

The American Association of Retired People (AARP) maintains a computerized Volunteer Talent Bank of over 8,500 members who want to volunteer. AARP matches the volunteer's skills and interests, contained in the Talent Bank, with AARP's needs and the needs of other national volunteer organizations across the nation, such as SCORE, the Red Cross, the National Park Service, and others.

Registering with the Volunteer Talent Bank (see Resources) is one way to find the volunteer position that fits your special needs. Anyone over the age of fifty is eligible to register.

Volunteering with something of value to do eases the shock of suddenly being removed from a lifetime of work. The National Retiree Volunteer Center (NRVC) acts as a consultant to corporations to educate and train company retirees for corporate programs, and to match their skills and interests for volunteering within the community. The structure of a formal organization, set up and run by retired employees, introduces retirees to volunteering at the beginning, when the shock is greatest.

The National Retiree Volunteer Center was established in 1986 with an advisory board including such experts on aging as Dr. Arthur Fleming, the former commissioner of aging and secretary of health; the late Rep. Claude Pepper, former chairman of the House Select Committee on Aging, and Jack Ossofsky, former head of the National Council on the Aging.

Honeywell, Pillsbury, General Mills, and Levi Strauss are some of the many companies utilizing NRVC to help their retired employees set up organizations for volunteering. For more information, contact the National Retiree Volunteer Center (see Resources).

Two major nationwide organizations are available to aid the retired executive in practicing executive skills in the volunteer arena. If you live in a metropolitan area, you'll find local chapters of the Executive Service Corps (ESC) and Service Corps of Retired Executives (SCORE) in the white pages of your phone book. If not, check with the national headquarters (see Resources).

There are twenty regional ESC organizations throughout the U.S., all members of the parent National Executive Service Corps. The National ESC was founded in 1977, tailored after the twenty-five-year-old International Executive Service Corps, which sends retired executives to short-term overseas assignments in developing countries.

Get Credit

A new system of volunteering is rapidly catching on. It's a service-credit approach. Volunteers gain time credits when volunteering that can later be spent when they need help. Edgar Cahn, a professor at the Columbia School of Law, started the movement with the aid of the Robert Wood Johnson Foundation. He convinced the foundation, an organization specializing in health-care grants, of the value of the service-credit concept. The foundation gave $1.2 million in grants for programs in San Francisco, Washington, D.C., Boston, Miami, St. Louis, and Brooklyn.

Sponsored volunteer organizations provide the health care services to help elders to remain in their homes longer. The following type services are provided: hospice care, individual care, household services, telephone reassurance, in-home visiting, hospital visiting, transportation, food shopping, escort, peer counseling, and language translation.

Participating volunteer organizations maintain each volunteer's hours of service in a computer data bank as credits for use later when needed. It's a program where time is the medium of exchange instead of dollars. People who have earned volunteer credits don't feel they are receiving charity when they spend their credits for similar help. Credits are cashed in by contacting a program manager. Volunteers like the program and program managers find the dropout rates are much lower than for conventional volunteer programs. For information about a service-credit volunteer program in your area, contact the Robert Wood Johnson Foundation (see Resources).

Executive Volunteers

Executives and upper-level managers have the most difficulty adjusting to retirement. They are no longer decision-makers holding the reins of power over dollars and people. The retired executive suffers a traumatic letdown. Such trauma has boosted the suicide rate to four times over that of the wage earner.

Volunteering can be the retired executive's safety net, an opportunity to practice executive talents through helping small businesses and non-profit organizations with their operational, organizational, and administrative problems.

SCORE, the Service Corporation of Retired Executives, is sponsored by the Small Business Administration. Founded in 1964, SCORE solicits successful retired business executives to volunteer their expertise for a full range of free management assistance to the small business community.

They counsel business owners and conduct workshops on such business functions as marketing, distributing, retailing, accounting, and inventory control. In the twenty-six years from 1964 to 1990, the SCORE ranks swelled to 11,750 volunteer executives. During 1990, they have held over 225,000 counseling sessions, lectured to over 125,000 participants, and presented over 3,000 small business workshops, all at a cost of only $2,500,000 a year for SCORE's nationwide programs.

Gorman Design Group, Inc., of Santa Rosa, California, is thankful for the SCORE volunteer management know-how. Partners Ray Gorman and Penny Bracken went to SCORE for advice on securing a Small Business Administration loan to pump financial blood into their tottering one-employee, two-partner ceramic jewelry manufacturing business.

They couldn't get a loan but the SCORE advisor recognized their true needs to be an effective marketing and sales plan. The partners implemented the SCORE counselor's suggestions, resulting in an increase of gross sales from $70,000 to $800,000 the first year. Three years later they had twenty-seven employees and their gross was $1,500,000.

Art Slope and his Rohnert Park, California, Village Shoe Repair business appreciates SCORE. "I had an eviction notice for rent nonpayment and my business was failing when I went to SCORE," Art said. "SCORE showed me how to save my business."

The SCORE counselor helped Art work out rent payments and improve sales by introducing a line of complementary shoe repair items, making the business profitable within five months. With continued advice from the SCORE counselor, Art's business eventually expanded to three stores and eighteen employees.

Herbert Baum joined SCORE in 1971. Since then he has progressed through every conceivable SCORE position of prominence. He is one of the few individuals to have a SCORE chapter named after him.

Mr. Baum is an eighty-nine-year-old dynamo who still puts in a day's work four days a week. Of all the volunteers I interviewed, he struck me as the most dedicated, active, and alert. One would never guess his age.

The Executive Service Corporation (ESC) is another nationwide organization of volunteer executives.

ESC volunteers consult with non-profit organizations for long-range planning, marketing, personnel management, facilities planning and construction, budgeting, finance and resource allocation, public relations and publications, and office practices and administration.

Once ESC has evaluated the non-profit client's needs and reviewed the ESC Project Committee appraisal report, it negotiates a consultation agreement with the client. If an agreement is reached, a team of ESC volunteer consultants studies the client's problems, then recommends management or program changes. The consultants are advisors only, and they do not compete with profit-oriented consulting firms.

The Contra Costa County Crime Prevention Committee, a non-profit agency organized to educate citizens in crime prevention, requested assistance in developing a long range financial and organizational plan. ESC volunteer Maurice Kohan worked directly with the committee to develop a plan that eventually resulted in a quadrupled budget and twenty-one neighborhood chapters, each with an adequate staff and volunteers to support the effort.

San Francisco's George Erb, a retired Safeway Stores executive, spent three months in Indonesia solving problems for a small group of grocery stores for the International Executive Service Corps.

Volunteer Teachers

Early man passed on his knowledge through stories and legends, handed down from one generation to the next, each building upon the other. You possess a lifetime of unique skills, experiences, and knowledge important to today's young people. You too can pass on your knowledge to younger generations, for today many educational volunteer organizations are begging for your help to teach our schoolchildren the knowledge they need.

Seniors Enriching Educational Roles (SEER) of San Francisco was founded in 1979. SEER's approximately 200 volunteers age sixty and older teach and tutor children from preschool through high school. Over 50 percent have been teaching for five years or longer. Only a small percentage were teachers by profession. They teach and tutor a variety of subjects such as math, history, and English as a second language. They also teach special skills during lunch and after school, conducting classes in knitting, dancing, fencing, jewelry making, and many other skills and hobbies. Their career-oriented lectures have been especially beneficial to high school students.

Other than age, SEER has only one other requirement to qualify. You must love children. Volunteers may register at the school in need of their teaching assistance or they can register directly with SEER, and that organization then finds a placement for their teaching services. Volunteers are expected to put in two hours or more a week.

Claire Herzog, SEER coordinator, started her volunteer teaching career working with the San Francisco Council of Jewish Women in 1977-78. One of the significant accomplishments of her volunteer teaching career was her initiation of a program at the Marina Junior High School, for emotionally disturbed students. Called the "Rap Room," the program operated under the guise of tutoring help, and successfully helped problem children before they got into serious trouble.

Betty Jean Beckman, a retired remedial math and reading teacher, used SEER volunteers to great advantage in her remedial classes. So, for the seven years following her retirement, she reciprocated by becoming a SEER volunteer herself. She runs a popular computer lab at William Cobb Elementary, for children from kindergarten through the fifth grade. The younger children gain early math and reading skills through interactive play with computer programs. The older children learn typing, word processing, graphics, and programming in the BASIC computer language. She uses volunteers to monitor the children's progress. To stimulate interest in learning, she initiated a program of using the computers for serious learning, followed by computer games – sort of like eating your peas before you get dessert.

SEER is a part of the San Francisco School Volunteers (see Resources). It is affiliated with the National Association of Partners in Education (see Resources).

The Retired Senior Volunteer Program (RSVP), a branch of ACTION, uses volunteers for teaching school children and older adults throughout the nation.

The Alliance, a Nebraska adult education program, uses RSVP volunteers on a regular basis to tutor students of all ages in learning the skills necessary to gain a GED high school diploma. They have successfully aided over 100 people each year to obtain a GED diploma. The U.S. Department of Education has recognized the program as one of the top ten adult basic education projects in a five-state region.

The RSVP volunteers in Crawford, Nebraska, initiated a living history program for schools and 4-H Clubs. The volunteers put on programs about earlier life in America. The program developed a strong link between the youth and older adults of the community.

Your own local community and recreation department probably wants retirees to teach adult courses. Hayward Area Recreation Department (HARD), of Hayward, California, is typical of most municipalities. HARD uses volunteers for teaching skills and hobbies to people enrolled in the HARD adult education programs. They usually have more than seventy volunteer instructors available to teach a variety of subjects. If you want to teach, HARD wants your help. If you have a unique skill, HARD will create a class for you to teach it.

Check the education systems in your area. Educators throughout the land are seeking volunteer help to educate both children and adults. Help stamp out illiteracy. Turn on the light of knowledge for others. Be a volunteer teacher.

Volunteer Associations

There are many other volunteer organizations that seek the assistance of retirees including Volunteer – The National Center (VNCC), Retired Senior Volunteer Program, National ESC, National Service Corps of Retired Executives (SCORE), and Seniors Enriching Educational Roles (SEER). See Resources for a complete listing of these organizations with addresses.

Volunteer Administration

Volunteering has fostered a new category of administrators filled with trainers, consultants, and managers, all dedicated to volunteer management. Volunteer service administration is recognized as a profession with its own ethics and standards. Opportunities abound in this field for retired executives who wish to once again become decision makers.

Volunteering is a career without pay. It's a career with the benefits of self-satisfaction, satisfying altruistic needs, exercising old skills, learning new skills, teaching others, and giving yourself the most important benefits of all: a reason for being, a feeling of self-worth, and a way to make a difference through helping others. Make your retirement the best it can be. Volunteer.

Bibliography

Barrett, James, and Geoffrey Williams. *Test Your Own Job Aptitude: Expand Your Career Potential.* New York: Penguin Books, 1981.

Bloomberg, Gerri, and Margaret Holden. *The Women's Job Search Handbook: Issues & Insights into the Workplace.* Charlotte, VT: Williamson Publishing, 1991.

Bolles, Richard Nelson. *What Color is Your Parachute?* Berkeley: Ten Speed Press, 1985.

Brabec, Barbara. *Homemade Money.* Whitehall, VA: Betterway Publications, Inc., 1986.

Catalyst staff. *Marketing Yourself: The Catalyst Women's Guide to Successful Resumes and Interviews.* New York: Putnam's Sons, 1980.

Catalyst staff. *What To Do With the Rest of Your Life.* New York: Simon & Schuster, 1980.

Cowle, Jerry. *How to Survive Getting Fired and Win.* New York: Warner Books, 1979.

Crockett, J.S. *For Those Who Sell . . . (and Who the Hell Doesn't?).* Farnsworth, 1974.

Douglass, Merrill E., and Donna N. *Manage Your Time, Manage Your Work, Manage Yourself.* New York: AMACOM, 1980.

Dychtwald, Ken, Ph.D., and Joe Flower. *Age Wave.* Los Angeles: Jeremy P. Tarcher, 1989.

Edwards, Paul, and Sarah. *Working From Home: Everything You Need to Know About Living and Working Under the Same Roof.* Los Angeles: Jeremy P. Tarcher, 1987.

Eyler, David R., Ph.D. *Starting & Operating a Home-Based Business.* New York: John Wiley & Sons, 1990.

Falvey, Jack. *What's Next? Career Strategies After 35.* Charlotte, VT: Williamson Publishing, 1987.

Figler, Howard. *The Complete Job-Search Handbook: All the Skills*

You Need to Get Any Job and Have a Good Time Doing It. New York: Holt, Rinehart & Winston, 1979.

Gale, Barry, and Linda. *Discover What You're Best At.* New York: Simon & Schuster, 1982.

Goldfein, Donna. *Every Woman's Guide to Getting Ready for the Right Career.* Millbrae, CA: Celestial Arts, 1981.

Holtz, Herman. *Advice, A High Profit Business: A Guide for Consultants and Other Entrepreneurs.* Englewood Cliffs, NJ: Prentice Hall, 1986.

——. *The Consultant's Guide to Winning Clients.* New York: John Wiley & Sons, 1988.

——. *Profit from Your Money-Making Ideas: How to Build a New Business or Expand an Existing One.* New York: American Management, 1980.

Hyatt, Carol. *Selling Yourself: The Woman's Selling Game.* New York: M. Evans, 1979.

Ingraham, Mark H. *My Purpose Holds: Reactions and Experiences in Retirement of TIAA-CREF Annuitants.* New York: Educational Research Division, Teachers Insurance and Annuity Association College Retirement Equities Fund, 1974.

Jehle, Faustin. *The Complete and Easy Guide to Social Security & Medicare.* Charlotte, VT: Williamson Publishing, annual.

Josefowitz, Natasha. *Paths to Power.* Menlo Park, CA: Addison-Wesley, 1980.

Kishel, Gregory F., and Patricia Gunter. *Cashing In on the Consulting Boom.* New York: John Wiley & Sons, 1985.

Lakein, Alan. *How To Get Control of Your Time and Your Life.* New York: Peter H. Wyden, 1973.

Lathrop, Richard. *Don't Use a Resume... Use a Qualifications Brief.* Berkeley: Ten Speed Press, 1980.

Levinson, Jay Conrad. *Earning Money Without a Job.* New York: Holt, Rinehart & Winston, 1979.

Lewis, William L. and Radlaurr. *How to Choose, Advance Your Career.* New York: Career Blazers Agency, 1983.

Maltz, Maxwell. *Psycho-Cybernetics.* New York: Grosset & Dunlap, 1970.

Marks, Edith, and Adel Lewis. *Job Hunting for the Disabled.* New York: Barron's Educational Series, 1983.

Marsh, DeLoss L. *Resumes That Get Interviews — Interviews That Get Offers.* Self-published, 1984.

Matzen, Robert. *Research Made Easy.* New York: Bantam, 1987.

Michelozzi, Betty Neville. *Coming Alive From 9 to 5.* Palo Alto: Mayfield Publishing, 1980.

Montgomery, Robert L. *How to Sell in 1980s—Successful Selling of Products, Services, and Ideas in a New Decade.* Englewood Cliffs, NJ: Prentice Hall, 1980.

Olsen, Nancy. *Starting a Mini-Business.* Sunnyvale, CA: Bear Flag Books, 1986.

Parker, Yana. *A Damn Good Resume Guide.* Berkeley: Parker & R, 1983.

Pepper, Terri P. and Nona D. *The New Entrepreneurs.* New York: Universe Books, 1980.

Pinson, Linda, and Jerry Jinnett. *The Home-Based Entrepreneur.* Tustin, CA: Out of Your Mind . . . And Into the Marketplace, 1989.

Shenson, Howard L. *How to Create & Market a Successful Seminar or Workshop.* Sarasota: The Consultant's Library, 1988.

Swell, Dr. Lila. *Success: You Can Make it Happen.* New York: Simon & Schuster, 1976.

Todd, Alden. *Finding Facts Fast.* Berkeley: Ten Speed Press, 1979.

U.S. Department of Labor, Bureau of Labor Statistics. Reprint from the Occupational Outlook Quarterly, Spring 1986. *The Job Outlook in Brief.* Washington: U.S. Government Printing Office, 1986.

Department of Labor, Employment and Training Administration. *Merchandising Your Job Talents.* Washington: U.S. Government Printing Office, 1986 (Revised).

Waymonn, Lynne. *Starting & Managing a Business From Your Home.* Washington: U.S. Small Business Administration, 1986.

Welch, Mary Scott. *Networking: The Great New Way for Women to Get Ahead.* New York: Harcourt Brace Jovanovich, 1980.

Willing, Jules Z. *The Reality of Retirement: The Inner Experience of Becoming a Retired Person.* New York: William Morrow, 1988.

Resources

Here is a listing of organizations, volunteer associations, and other resources.

Behaviordyne, 994 San Antonio Road, Palo Alto, CA 94303 (415-857-0111). Offers Strong-Campbell Interest Inventory, $25.

Chronicle Guidance Publications, P.O. Box 1190, Moravia, NY 13118 (315-497-0330). Offers self-administered aptitude tests, $27.50.

Educational Testing Service, Princeton, NJ 08541.

Elderhostel, 80 Boylston St. Suite 400, Boston, MA 02116.

ESC. Executive Service Corps, 257 Park Avenue South, New York, NY 10010 (212-529-6660).

Howard L. Shenson, CMC, 20750 Ventura Blvd., Woodland Hills, CA 91364 (818-703-1415). Educational packages on consulting.

International Correspondence Schools (ICS), a subsidiary of the National Education Corporation, 925 Oak Street, Scranton, PA 18515.

John C. Crystal Center, 111 E. 31st St., New York, NY 10016.

Johnson O'Connor Research Foundation (212-838-0550).

Lifelong Learning Independent Study, University of California Extension, 2223 Fulton Street, Berkeley, CA 94720 (415-642-4124). Catalog on over 200 courses.

Locum Tenens, Inc. Eastern region: 400 Perimeter Center Terrace, Suite 760, Atlanta, GA 30346 (404-393-1210). Western region:

4600 South Ulster Street, Suite 680, Denver, CO 80237 (303-850-7030).

National Association of Partners in Education, 601 Wythe Street, Suite 200, Alexandria, VA 22314.

National Association of Temporary Services (NATS), 119 South Saint Asaph St., Alexandria, VA 22314 (703-549-6287).

National Retiree Volunteer Center, 607 Marquette Ave., Suite 10, Minneapolis, MN 55402 (612-341-2689).

Operation Able (Ability Based on Long Experience), 36 S. Wabash Ave., Chicago, IL 60603

Psychological Assessment Resources, P.O. Box 998, Odessa, FL 33556 (813-968-3003). Offers John Holland's Self-Directed Search, $5.50

Robert Wood Johnson Foundation, P.O. Box 2316, Princeton, NJ 08543-2316 (609-452-8701). Service-credit volunteer program information.

RSVP. Retired Senior Volunteer Program (part of ACTION Volunteer Agency), 806 Connecticut Ave. NW, Room M1006, Washington, DC 20525 (202-634-9359).

SBIR Pre-Solicitation Announcements, Small Business Administration, 1441 L Street NW, Washington, DC 20416.

SCORE. Service Corps of Retired Executives, 1825 Connecticut Ave. NW, Suite 503, Washington, DC 20009. (202-653-6279).

SEER. Seniors Enriching Educational Roles. Part of the San Francisco School Volunteers, 340 Pine Street, Third Floor, San Francisco, CA 94104 (415-274-0257).

Volunteer Talent Bank, 1909 K Street NW, Washington, DC 20049.

Volunteer – The National Center (VNCC), (703-276-0542).

Work Force Education, AARP Worker Equity Department, 1909 K Street NW, Washington, DC 20049.

The Writer, 120 Boylston St., Boston, MA 02116.

Writer's Digest, 1507 Dana Ave., Cincinnati, OH 45207.

More good books from
WILLIAMSON PUBLISHING

To order additional copies of *Retirement Careers,* please enclose $10.95 per copy plus $2.00 shipping and handling. Follow "To Order" instructions on the last page. Thank you.

THE COMPLETE AND EASY GUIDE TO SOCIAL SECURITY & MEDICARE
by Faustin F. Jehle

A lifesaver of a book for every senior citizen – in fact every citizen – you know. Do someone a special favor, and give this book as a gift. Written in "plain English," here's all that red tape unravelled. Over 300,000 copies sold!

175 pages, 8¹/2 × 11, charts and tables,
Quality paperback, $10.95

WHAT'S NEXT?
Career Strategies After 35
by Jack Falvey

Falvey explodes myths right and left and sets you on a straight course to a satisfying and successful mid-life career. Bring an open mind to his book and you'll be on your way. A liberating book to help us all get happily back into work.

192 pages, 6 × 9
Quality paperback, $9.95

THE WOMEN'S JOB SEARCH HANDBOOK
Issues and Insights into the Workplace
by Gerri Bloomberg and Margaret Holden

Delves into the issues that keep women of all ages out of the jobs they want and deserve . . . and often out of the workplace entirely. They tell it like it is – not like we may wish it were. Covers your initial mindset, turning volunteer work into bona fide work experience, reentering the job market after many years at home, where to start. With this book, if you want to work at a job you love, you can do it!

252 pages
Quality paperback, $12.95

INTERNATIONAL CAREERS
An Insider's Guide
by David Win

If you long for a career that combines the excitement of foreign lifestyles and markets, the opportunity to explore your potential, the promise of monetary and personal reward, then learn from David Win how to get off the stateside corporate ladder and into the newly emerging areas of international careers. Now's the time!

224 pages, 6 × 9, charts and sources
Quality paperback, $10.95

AFTER COLLEGE
The Business of Getting Jobs
by Jack Falvey

Wise and wonderful . . . don't leave college without it. Filled with unorthodox suggestions (avoid campus recruiters at all costs!), hands-on tools (put your money in stationery, not in resumes), wise observations (grad school? – why pay to learn what others are paid to learn better). This is a job-search book with a real difference that will make a real difference in your life no matter what your age!

192 pages, 6 × 9
Quality paperback, $9.95

Best Strategies for a Job Going Sour
by Stephen Cohen, MD

Whether rumor has it that your whole department is about to be eliminated or you just have that sinking feeling that things will never get better between you and your boss, here is the one book that will help you save your job (if that's what you want), or leave on your own terms. All about how to avoid being victimized, how to read the writing on the wall, how to know what are real opportunities, and how to avoid dead-end promotions. Take your work life back into your own hands!

192 pages, 6 × 9
Quality paperback, $10.95

THE BROWN BAG COOKBOOK
Nutritious Portable Lunches for Kids and Grown-Ups
by Sara Sloan

Here are more than 1,000 brown bag lunch ideas with 150 recipes for simple, quick, nutritious lunches that kids will love. Breakfast ideas, too! This popular book is now in its sixth printing!

192 pages, 8¹/4 × 7¹/4, illustrations
Quality paperback, $8.95

GOLDE'S HOMEMADE COOKIES
by Golde Soloway

Over 50,000 copies of this marvelous cookbook have been sold with 135 of the most delicious cookie recipes imaginable. *Publishers Weekly* says, "Cookies are her chosen realm and how sweet a world it is to visit." You're sure to agree! Golde's fans order her book over and over to give to friends and family . . . it's that good!

162 pages, 8¹/4 × 7¹/4, illustrations
Quality paperback, $8.95

CARING FOR OLDER CATS & DOGS
Extending Your Pet's Healthy Life
by Robert Anderson, DVM and Barbara J. Wrede

Here's the only book that will help you distinguish the signs of natural aging from pain and suffering, that will help you care for your pet with compassion and knowledge. How to help your older pet, how to nourish, nurture, and nurse your cat or dog, and finally when and how to let go. Medically sound with reasonable homeopathic remedies too, mixed with practical advice and compassion.
Every older pet deserves an owner who has read this!

192 pages, 6 × 9, illustrations
Quality paperback, $10.95

To Order:
At your bookstore or order directly from Williamson Publishing. We accept Visa and MasterCard (please include number and expiration date), or send check to:

Williamson Publishing Company
Church Hill Road, P.O. Box 185
Charlotte, Vermont 05445
Toll-free phone orders with credit cards:
1-800-234-8791

Please add $2.00 for postage and handling. Satisfaction is guaranteed or full refund without questions or quibbles.

Distributed by

CAREER RESEARCH & TESTING
2005 Hamilton Ave., Suite 250
San Jose, California 95125
(408) 559-4945